# Ethan Murrow

# Ethan Murrow

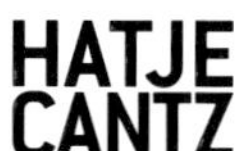

# Introduction

Ethan Murrow

Kalaloch Lodge sits on a rough coastline in the Pacific Northwest, part of the Olympic National Park. A decade ago, I was entering the lodge restaurant and discovered a photo of my great-grandparents from the exact same site. In the grainy image, they stand among their logging camp kitchen garden, looking stoic and overworked. I began to sand away at the sheen of the story of their American Dream and the camps they worked in, which were filled with labor strife, impoverishment, and bits and pieces of hard won success. The sheer scope of what happened in the West as populations from the East pushed to the margins of North America is a staggering history of discovery, ignorance, reinvention, loss, and the harsh transformation of a landscape and people. This narrative and the factual, idealized, absurd, and uncomfortable ways in which we Americans choose to craft tales about our country has defined what I navigate.

Many of the photographs, paintings, and films that deal with the early history of the United States are saturated with ideas of false hope and impossible perfection. The country is particularly good at rendering a vision of itself that conveniently edits out the messy, unwanted, and uncomfortable truths of our past. The Hudson River School painter Albert Bierstadt, for example, created a grand version of America that was part reality, part heroic invention, and full of a colonial, power-hungry view of the country. Bierstadt has been a frequent target of admiration as well as cynical reference in the drawings.

I nod to these masterworks, recognizing that the ambition and possibility of the United States can be seen within these depictions of drama and wonder. Many are resampled and coagulated with individuals and moments that are at odds with the whitewashed sublime. Through a mash up of images, I hope to cut away at the neat and tidy narrative of progress and domination and create moments that deal with the abundant misinformation, deep confusion, genuine absurdity, and billowing mass that has always kept this country on its toes.

As our world leaks and creaks forward, landscape can act as the ultimate term and representation of the joys and foibles of our actions. Landscape is an aesthetic ideal, an edited view of reality that suits the maker—in essence, a fiction. For me, the word has come to define our use of images and stories to convince ourselves of who we are, what we know to be true, and what we wish was fact.

These drawings are re-tellings of histories, past images, heroes, and idiots. They are obsessively detailed puzzles and scenarios intended to honor a lineage of grand gestures and soapboxing and expose the deficiencies and dangers of doing so in the first place.

*Pluto* Installation view

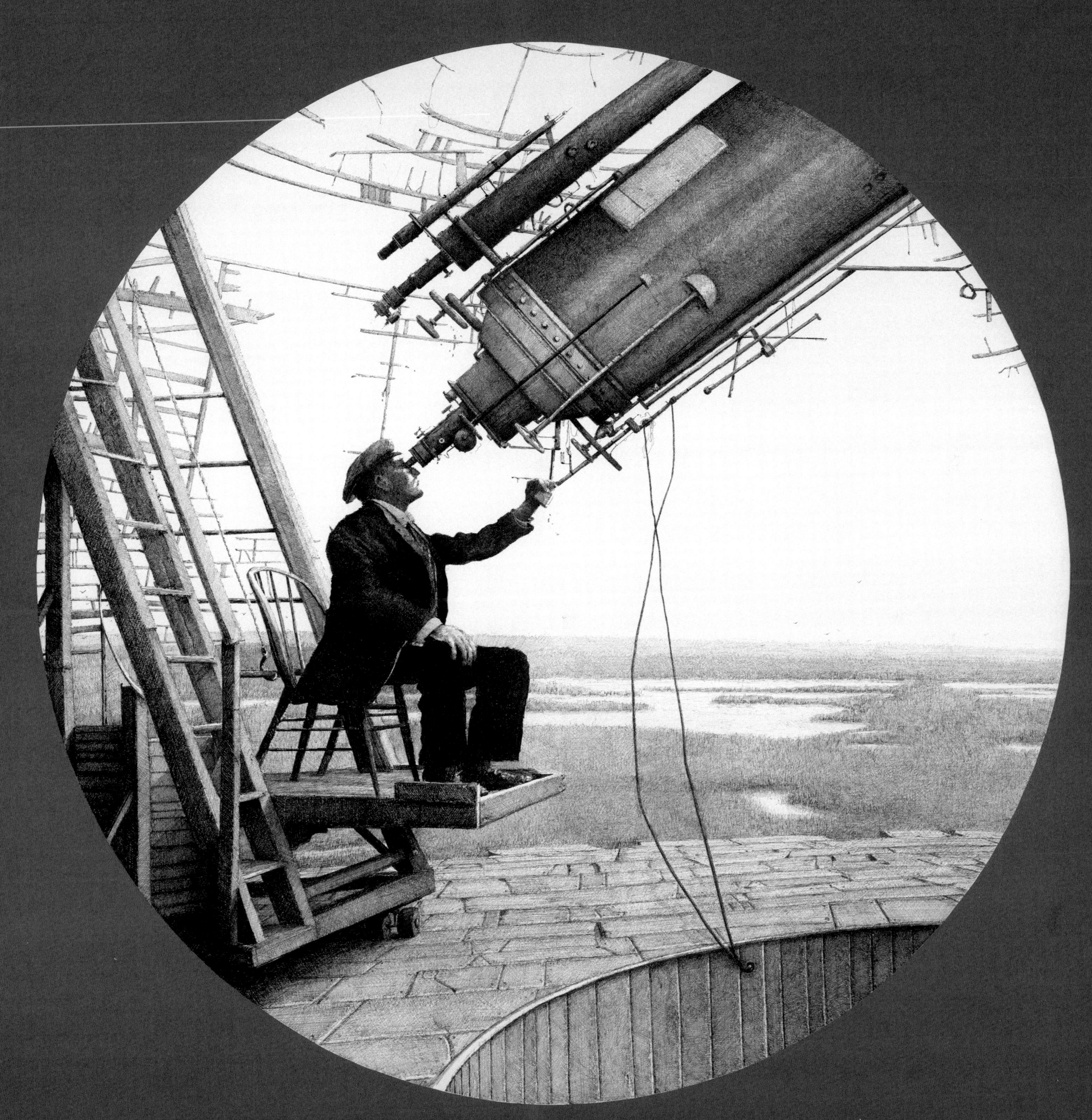

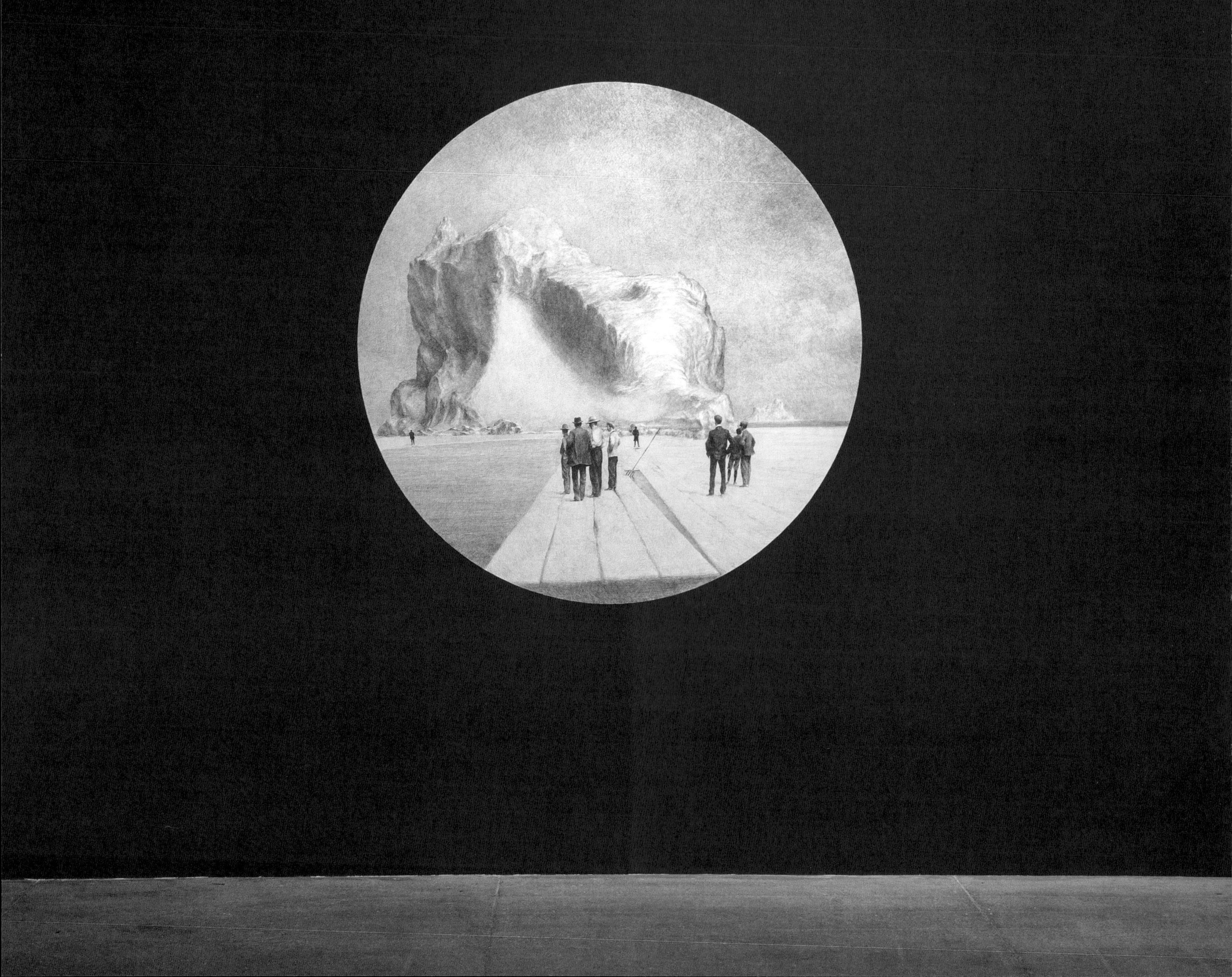

# The One and the Many

Ruth Erickson
Assistant Curator, Institute of Contemporary Art, Boston

## Walls as Drawings

A consummate storyteller and avid experimenter, Ethan Murrow has worked in painting, photography, film, sculpture, and drawing to explore the narrow margins between fact and fiction, idiocy and ingenuity, dignity and depravity, especially as they emerge in human behavior and American history. While Murrow is best known for graphite-on-paper drawings—often created in a series to explore an idea—in recent years, he has developed a new genre of work that is increasingly occupying a central position in his practice: wall drawings.

Murrow first put a ballpoint pen to a wall in 2010 as a lark. The exhibition, *Will Be Snaring Meteorites* (Winston Wächter, Seattle), featured a series of graphite-on-paper drawings that portrayed a female character as a wily amateur astronomer reaching for, measuring, and sometimes capturing, by net or by hand, Nerf balls interloping as meteorites. One sphere appears to have escaped her grasp and the confines of the paper's edges. At the upper edge of the gallery wall, Murrow drew the lower portion of a funny looking orb, as if to suggest it was floating out of the gallery space. At the bottom edge of the wall, he drew a very small figure from behind. The composition implied a huge expanse of space between floor and ceiling, one that has no relation to the actual built space but one that nonetheless used the architecture to render this allusion. It is perhaps this relation to architecture—to its histories, space, and experiences—that most distinguishes Murrow's wall drawings from his graphite-on-paper work. In an era before the invention of paper or pencil, in the caves of southern France, walls were the very first surfaces that humans marked. Since these early scenes of flora and fauna drawn on the sides of cave dwellings, the wall has been a rich surface for a wide range of marks and materials, from the frescos of the Renaissance to the wild style lettering of 1980s graffiti writers. Though for a long period, let's call it the modern era, the wall was largely a passive entity, something to hold what was being presented, and, in that supporting position, largely invisible. Artists began to turn their attention to the wall again in the middle of the twentieth century, when a desire to reveal the support structures of art—whether the stretcher of the painted canvas, the economies of the market, or the institutional relationships of museums—captured the attention of many practitioners. Artists measured gallery walls (Mel Bochner), propped sculptures on them (Richard Serra), pierced through them (Vito Acconci), cast them (Rachel Whiteread), and integrated them into complex installations. These artists demonstrated a renewed interest in grounding their works in real time and space—of the exhibition and museum, neighborhood, and society. The wall, especially as it separates inside from outside, demarcating the realm of art from that of non-art, became a prime target for contemporary artists.

At its most basic function, the wall connects floor to ceiling, creating an essential structural plane that is usually fixed in space. Drawings on walls accrue countless attributes from this close connection to architecture, whether tying into specific histories of a building, room, or site, or reacting to their contemporary uses. The locatedeness of drawings on these architectural elements is quite distinct from the commerce and the movement of discrete, framed, and saleable works and endows them with a subtle resistance to market forces. Once completed, wall drawings become part of the fabric of the building, most often painted over to make way for the next project. They exist in the space between drawing, architecture, and the time-based media of performance. To work on walls frequently means to work in the view of a public and even for a public.

Another characteristic of wall drawings is their appeal to human perception. After all, human perspective is fundamentally rooted in the erect posture assumed by humans during evolution, a posture that has shaped how humans see and make sense of space. The verticality of the wall, thus, corresponds to the vertical orientation of human viewers, compelling a certain affinity between that structure and the body. By virtue of this close association with the phenomenological experience of humans, such drawings present an opportunity to manipulate vision and perspective. Murrow has exploited all of these aspects of wall drawings over the past five years, harnessing their capacity to bring into dialogue the architecture and public of the museum with the art on view. This essay traces a line through Murrow's ever-evolving oeuvre to examine a series of increasingly ambitious wall works undertaken by the artist that pose important questions about vision, society, and history.

## Walls as Doubles

Murrow made drawings on walls to accompany a series of solo exhibitions beginning in 2011, using their surface to expand upon thematic threads in the exhibitions. In *Doppler Doppelganger* (Winston Wächter, New York, 2011), described by Murrow as "a search for a double or an echo of oneself," the wall seems to be the perfect kind of double for the paper works that hang on it. Depicting characters seeking, often through sonic means, someone or something that offers a double of the self—a doubling that produces, at once, recognition and estrangement. Upon entering the gallery, visitors were first greeted by a contraption of cones and speakers suspended in air by a kind of net. This *Listening Device*, as the drawing was titled, suggestively invites viewers to put ear to wall, listening for sounds—whether familiar or unfamiliar—that might trigger a discovery of the self in the other. In doing so, the wall drawing solicits visitors to mimic the behavior of the drawn figures, who bring sundry devices to ear in uncertain and probably ill-fated searches for echoes of the self. Through *Listening Device*, Murrow broadens the

*Doodlebugging* Installation view

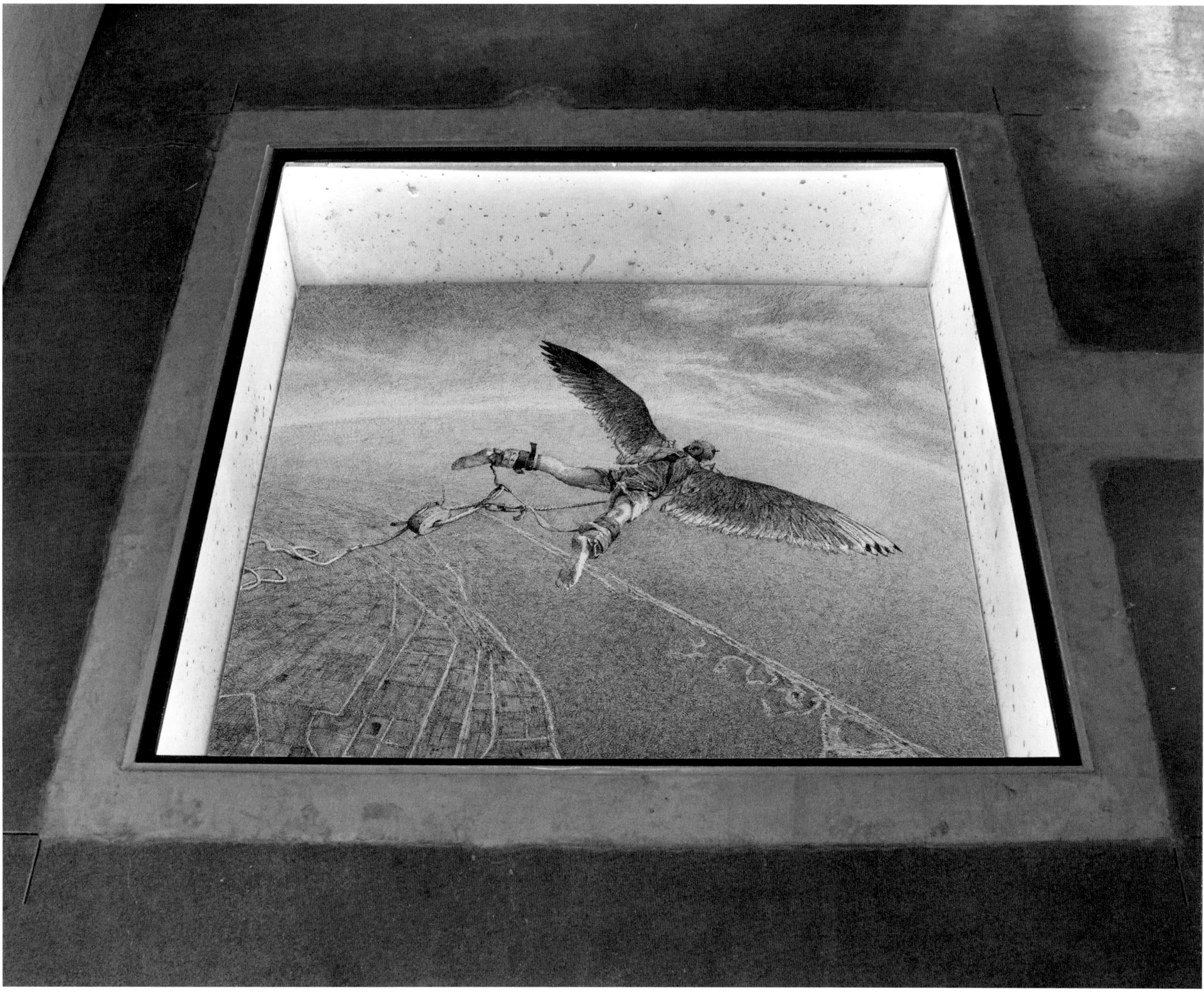

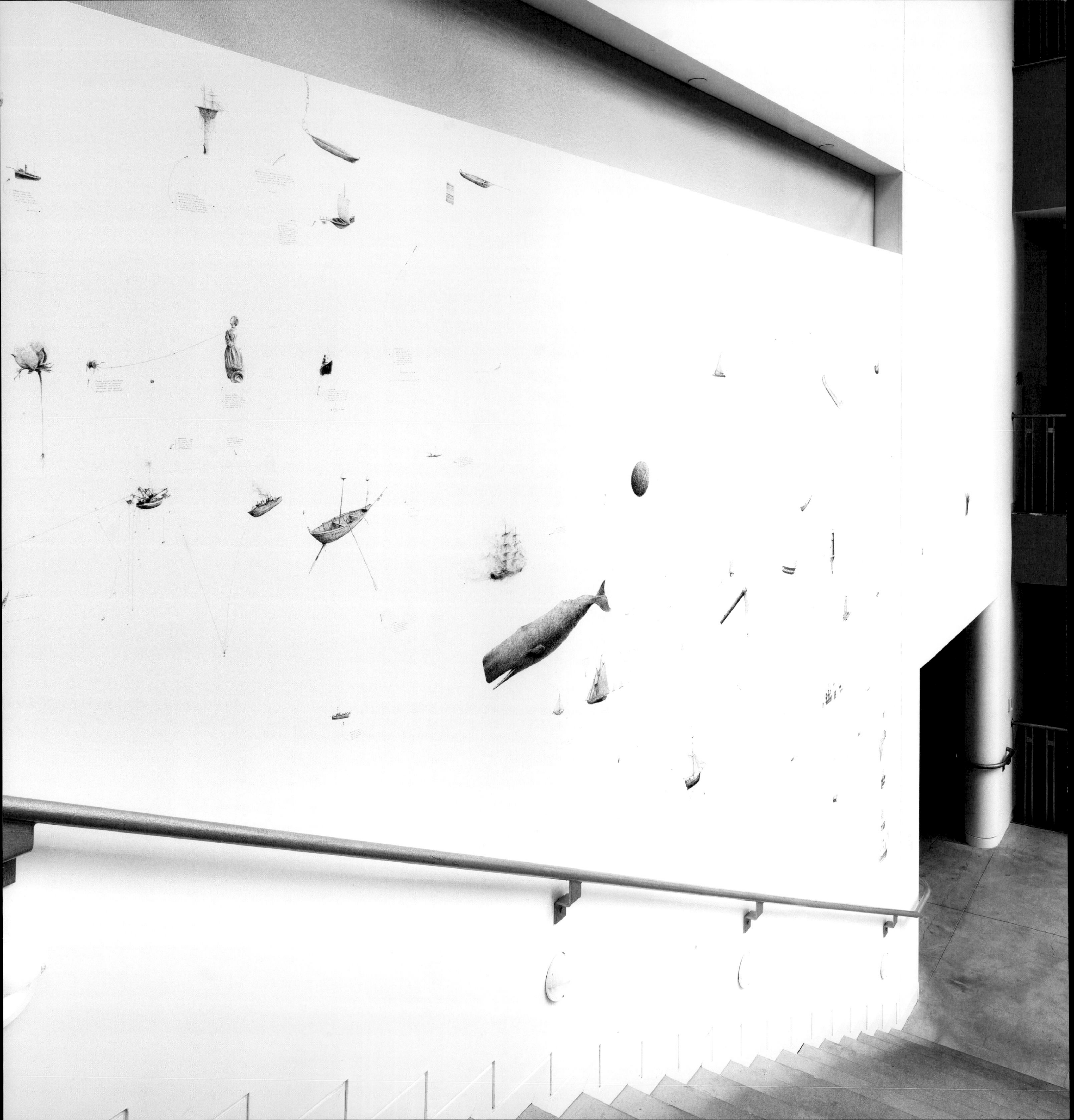

exhibition's conceptual thrust by initiating acts of doubling within the gallery space and the narrative of the exhibition. In *Positions of Power, Land View* (The Clay Center, Charleston, West Virginia, 2013), Murrow sketched three large-scale wall drawings in ballpoint pen that extended the exhibition's inquiry into aerial surveillance.

The drawings depicted three imaginary structures—part scaffold, silo, platform, and ladder—that reached up from the floor, down from the ceiling, or out from the wall into pictorial space. These unpopulated constructions extended to the edges of built space, suggestively moving beyond the confines of the gallery and ground to offer views from above. The surrounding drawings on paper and sculptural work presented engrossing views from elevated perspectives, which drew inspiration from the majestic landscapes of the Hudson River School painters, the detailed maps of government cartographers, and the ocular devices of military surveyors. Placed within this context, the wall drawings tied the content of the exhibition to the space of the gallery and to the experiences of visitors. The "position of power" was no longer just the unidentified and omniscient one of linear perspective but also the individual and embodied ones of visitors. By drawing in the shared architectural space of viewers, Murrow is able to involve and implicate them more directly in the ideas and experiences he so deftly depicts within the rectilinear frame of the works on paper.

*Flotilla* Installation view

## Walls as Experiences

The experiential aspects of drawings on walls as it relates to architecture deepened with Murrow's expansive work *Flotilla* (deCordova Museum and Sculpture Park, 2013). Commissioned for the 2013 deCordova Biennial, this drawing consisted of 120 smaller drawings of watercraft from throughout the history of the United States. Sited on a three-story wall adjacent to a grand staircase leading to the museum's galleries, the drawing functioned as a kind of map or atlas, linking individual vessels to chart explicit and implicit relationships between, for instance, slavery and commerce or the Vikings and the east coast. Thus, the iconic *Mayflower* that transported pilgrims to the New World in 1620 connects by a thin drawn line to boats used in the emigration of Cubans to the US in the 1980s. While each vessel drills down to a particular moment in history, the entire vast work pictures time by tracing human navigation on the seas. The site of the drawing compels a gradual experience of it, which closely relates to its composition and structure. As visitors mount the stairs, they unravel the histories embedded into the map, line-by-line, step-by-step. The shifting light of the sun streaming through an opposing wall of windows bathes the wall work in a subtle, moving light evocative of the watery subject and of the ever-changing status of history and its interpretation. *Flotilla* was the first wall drawing that Murrow created as a standalone work, and since completing it, he has undertaken numerous important commissions of such works, which he plans and executes to be increasingly responsive to the specificities of site. A permanent drawing—done for the first time in permanent marker—at the headquarters of a technology company in Cambridge, addresses the history of innovation in Kendall Square, where it is located, and the shaping of the neighboring Charles River. At Winston Wächter in Seattle, Murrow installed *Doodlebugging* (2015), a permanent marker drawing on wood of a winged figure diving toward a distant landscape into a depression in the floor. Lit from within and covered with glass, the installation invites viewers to stand over the drawing, to match its dramatic perspectival view, which is both riveting and vertigo inducing. Even temporary wall drawings have increasingly picked up on aspects particular to the sites of their execution.

*Agglomerate* (Slete Gallery, Los Angeles, 2015) depicts a long line of men hiking up the white gallery wall, which serves as a snowy mountain—an escape route, a retreat—in an exhibition about the inevitable climate changes that are upon us. *Portmanteau* (Children's Museum of the Arts, New York, 2015) depicts the magician Houdini, whose bag has opened to reveal a wonderfully eclectic set of objects spread across the wall, a field of images for the museum's young visitors to discover in a scavenger-like fashion. With each project, Murrow discerns new ways of opening his drawing to the spaces and the publics of each site, inviting the collaboration of many hands and ideas to produce a truly public art.

## Walls as Responses

Murrow's most recent wall drawing, *Seastead* (Institute of Contemporary Art, Boston, 2015), responds to the site of the museum with an open and unresolvable question: Is this a beginning or an ending? On a large wall painted dark gray in the museum's glass lobby, Murrow drew a round oculus to focus attention on a dramatic scene of a large boat hauling a massive cathedral into an otherwise vast and empty sea. The cathedral—a traditional basilica with central, high dome (easily mistaken as the US Capitol)—sits askew on the flat top of the liner. This slightly precarious position suggests the church may have been hastily loaded onto the boat, perhaps due to duress or carelessness. Is this an attempt to save the cathedral from destruction, or to dispose of it? In the upper right, a single figure dangles from the untethered ropes of a hot air balloon. Is he escaping by air or attempting to reach the boat below? The scene is enigmatic, the vista sublime, and the effort immense.

The landscape around the ICA seems to be in a state of constant change. New buildings appear over night, while historical structures, like the brick sailor's church, Our Lady of Good Hope, disappear just as quickly. This dramatic architectural transformation of the Seaport District (what has already taken place and what is planned for the near future) is only echoed in the watery depths of the adjoining Boston Harbor. While the sea's steady tides might suggest a sense of timelessness—the retreat and return with each

*Flotilla* Installation view

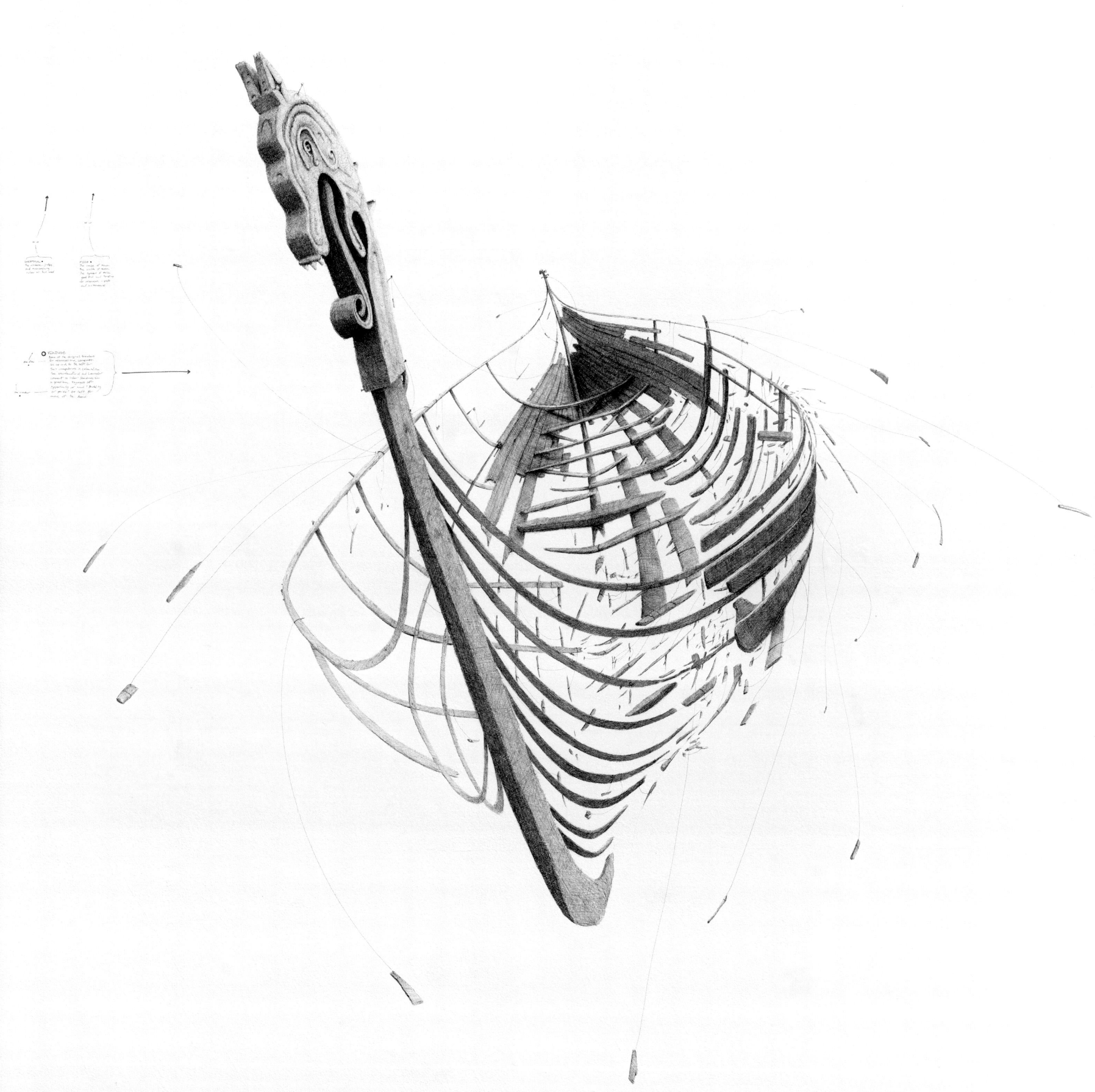
VIKINGS

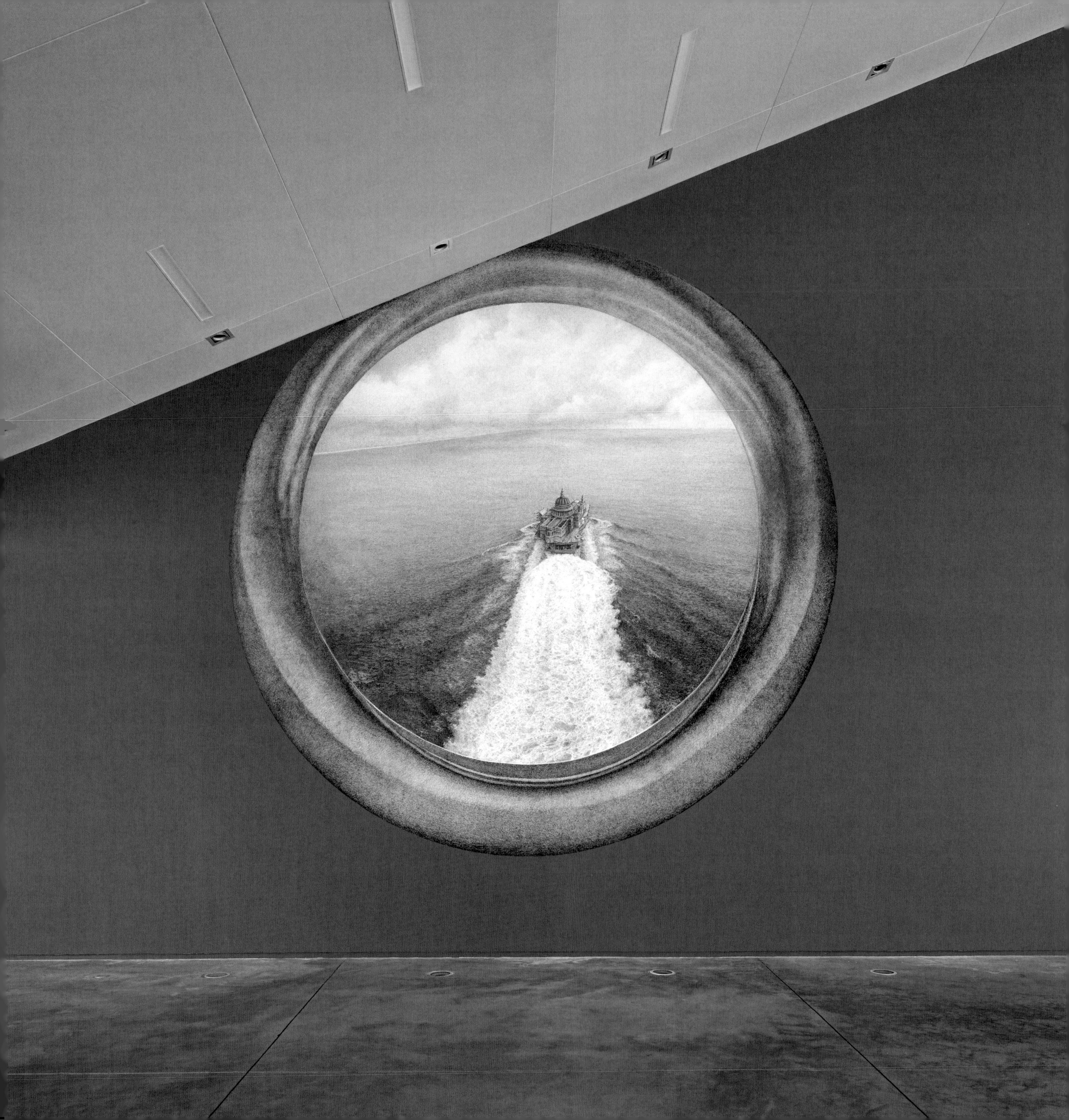

moon cycle—the natural harbor links to a vast network of waterways, bodies, and commerce undergoing significant alterations. The harbor becomes a kind of marker of the many ways that environmental changes, from rising sea levels to diminished fishing stocks, reshape, and will increasingly reshape, human existence on the earth. It is with these thoughts in mind that I invited Murrow to create a wall drawing for the ICA's Sandra and Gerald Fineberg Art Wall.

Murrow based his drawing of the large boat on American aircraft carriers, the impressive nautical devices that have been central to the nation's military prowess. Perched on top of the carrier, Murrow has drawn St. Paul's Cathedral, which was constructed in London after the great fire in 1666 and withstood the Blitz bombing of World War II. Sourcing images from the Internet, Murrow created a digital mock-up, marrying the carrier and the cathedral in the middle of the sea, and then set out with three assistants to draw it, by hand and in marker, directly on the wall over the course of ten days. This formidable task, which took almost 100 hours and exhausted over 400 Sharpie pens, embodied a remarkable commitment and expenditure of raw energy, an effort that resonated with the subject matter.

Structures of immense physical strength, the carrier and cathedral are symbolic of the nations that created them—not coincidentally, the same great powers of Boston's own Puritan origins—but in *Seastead*, they appear somewhat tenuous. Is this a rebellious breakaway, a forced exile, or a utopian endeavor? What triggered it? Insurgent political regimes, rising sea levels? The work's title, *Seastead*, is derived from "seasteading" (a combination of the words "sea" and "homesteading"), which refers to the creation of an island state outside of the boundaries and the laws of any sovereign nation. If taken at face value, the title and imagery may conjure a break-up of the great Western powers and the formation of a new entity in its nascent stage of assembly, an apt characterization of the twenty-first century. Such a process is replicated in the individual marks that begin as countless crosshatches by a team of hands and then cohere at a distance into a photorealistic drawing only to dissolve into thousands of indeterminable marks upon scrutiny. Murrow holds together these opposing processes, allowing formation and disintegration to coexist in both the narrative arc and drawing. *Seastead* is neither a beginning nor an ending, but rather both at once, capturing the resilience of the one and the many working together.

*Seastead* Installation view

# Omniscient Landscapes

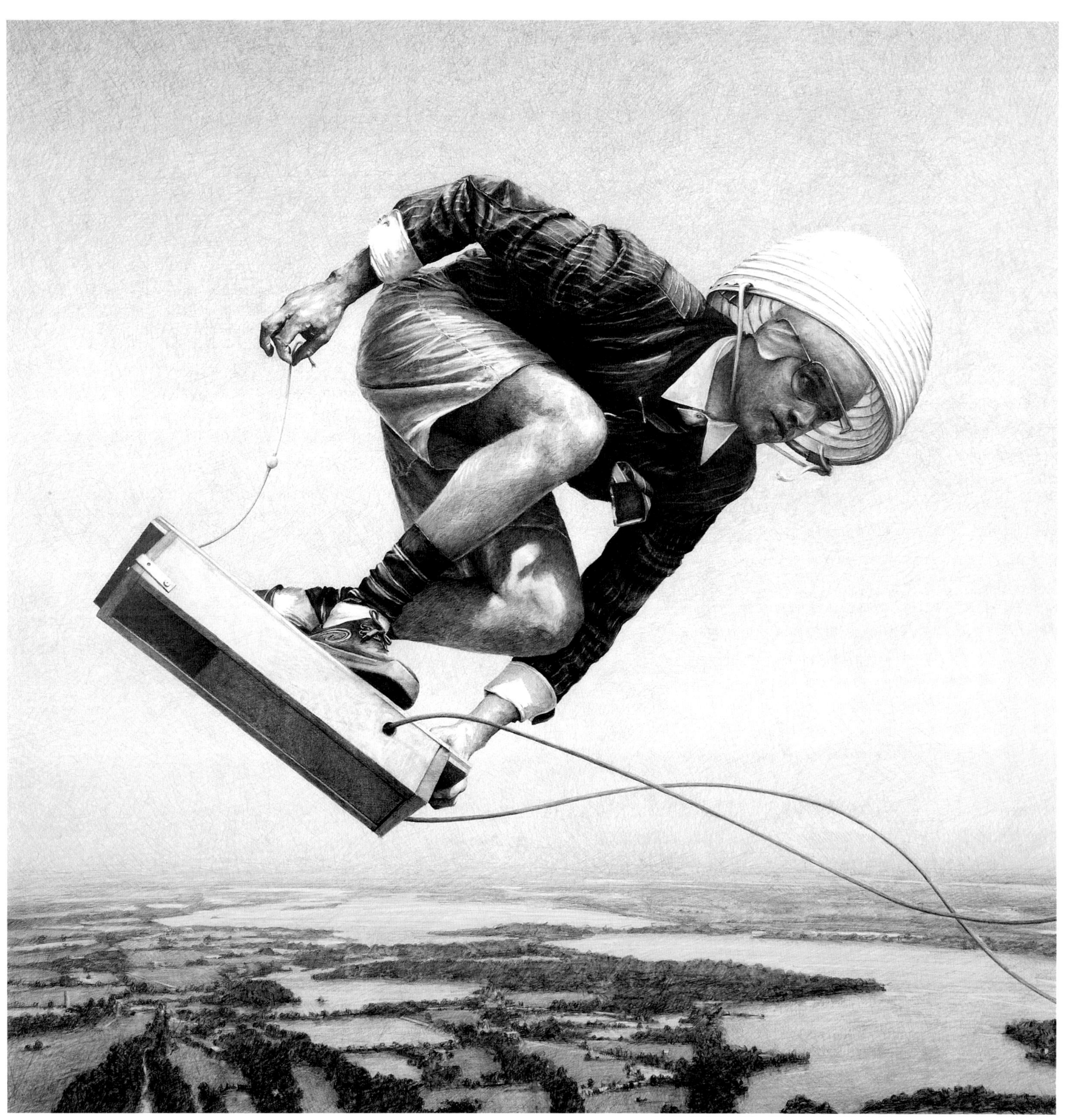

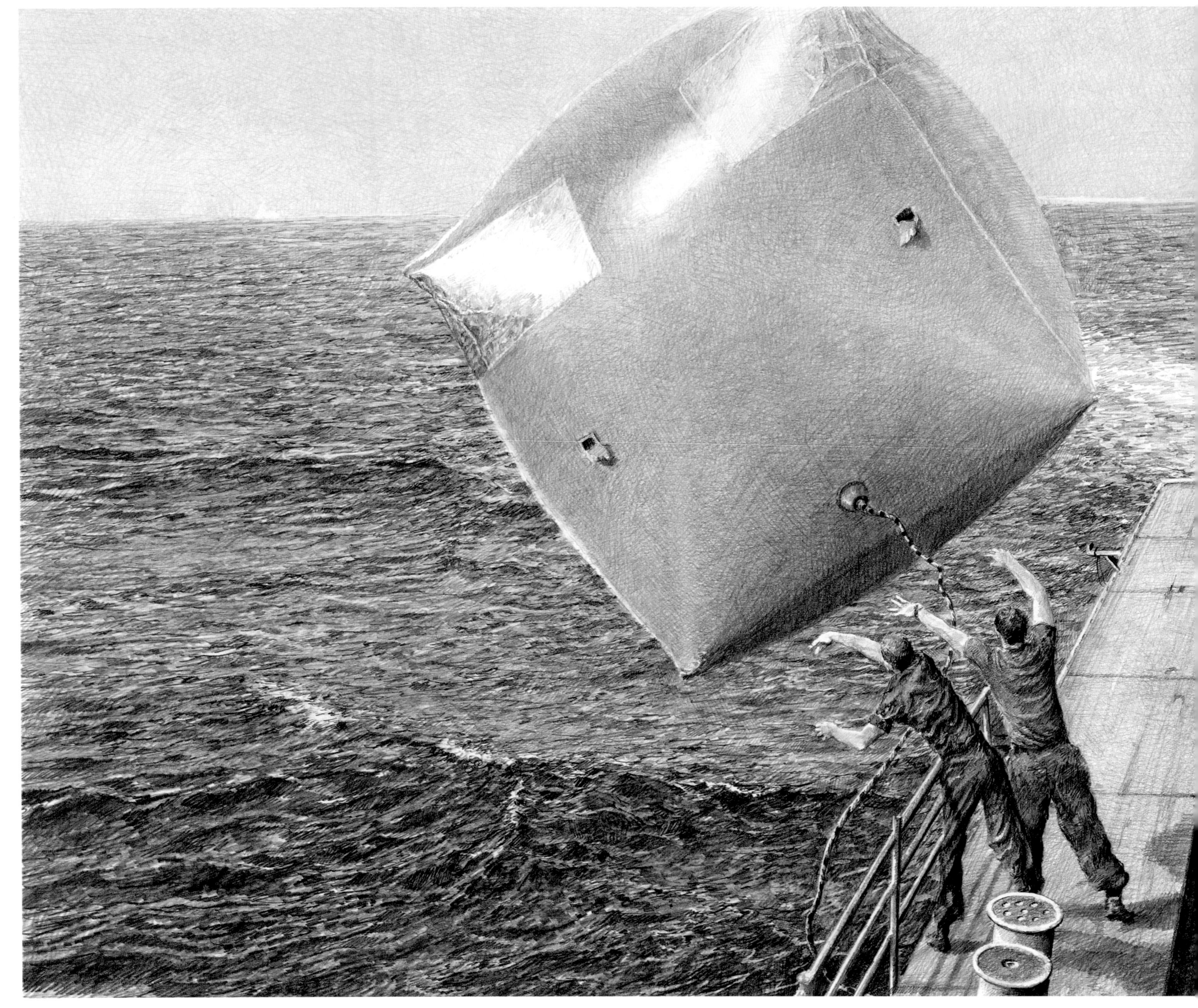

Previous page:
*Sled Is Responsive, Soft Landing in Doubt*

*Northwest Passage*

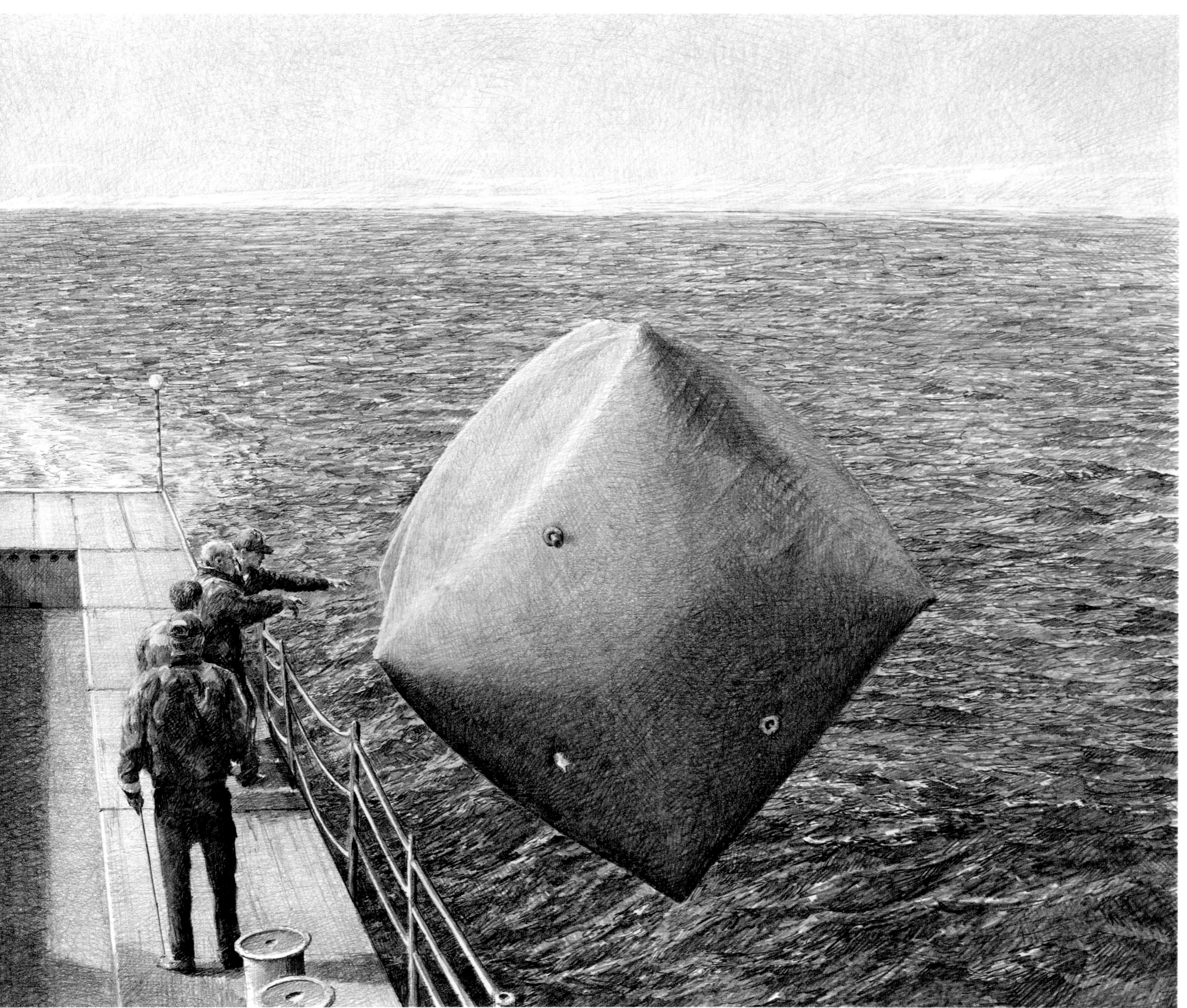

*Foot Is Still Cramping Up, Results Otherwise Positive*

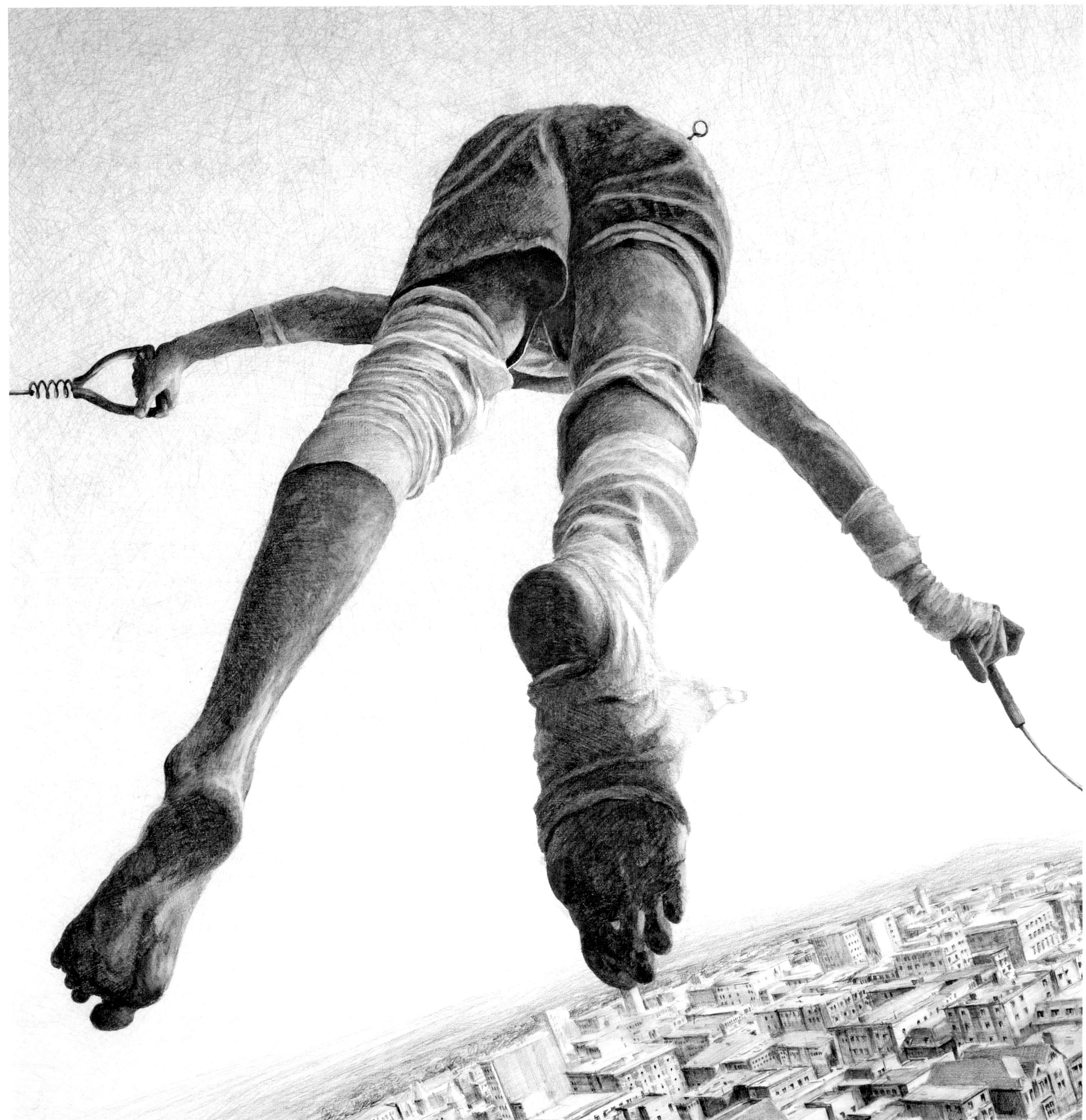

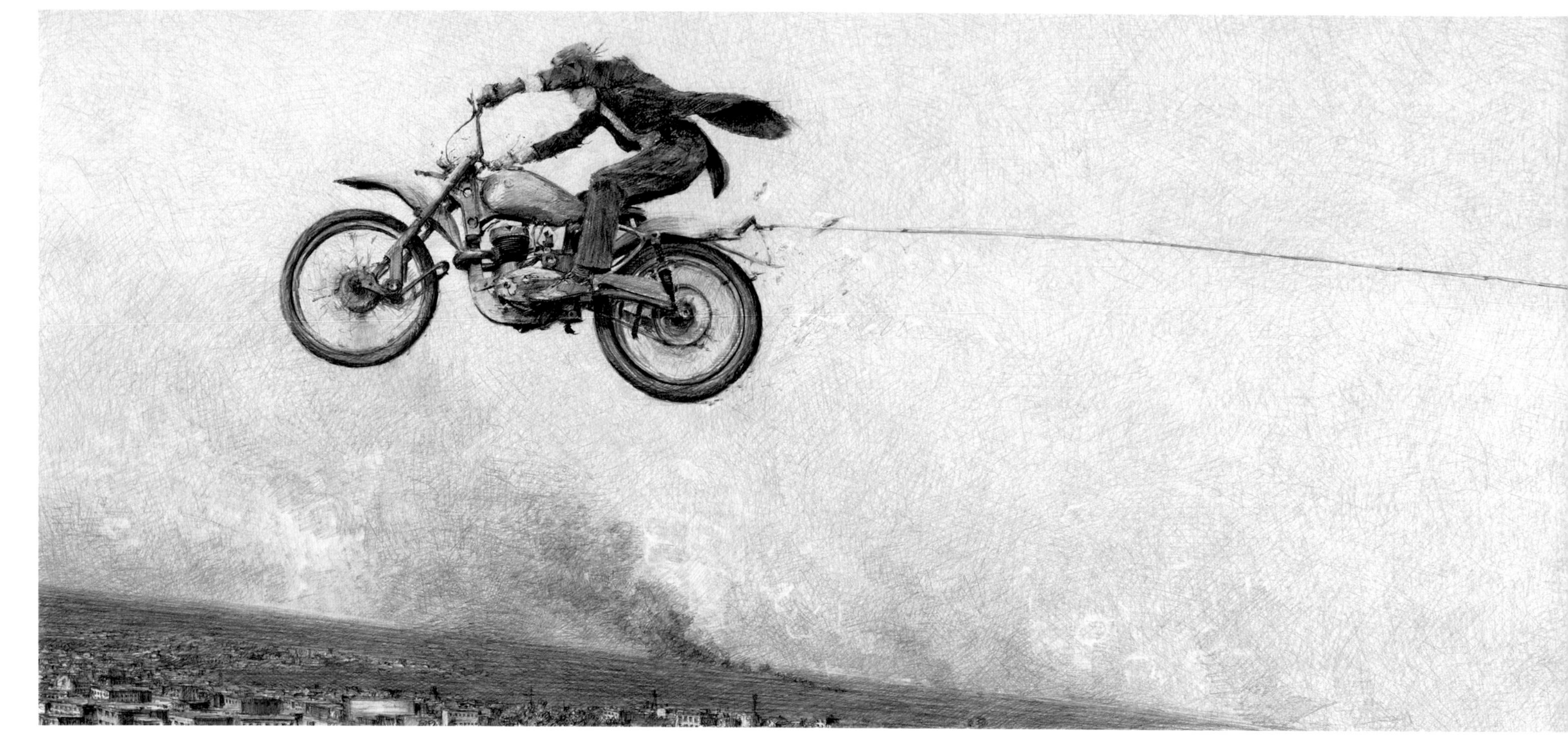

Exit

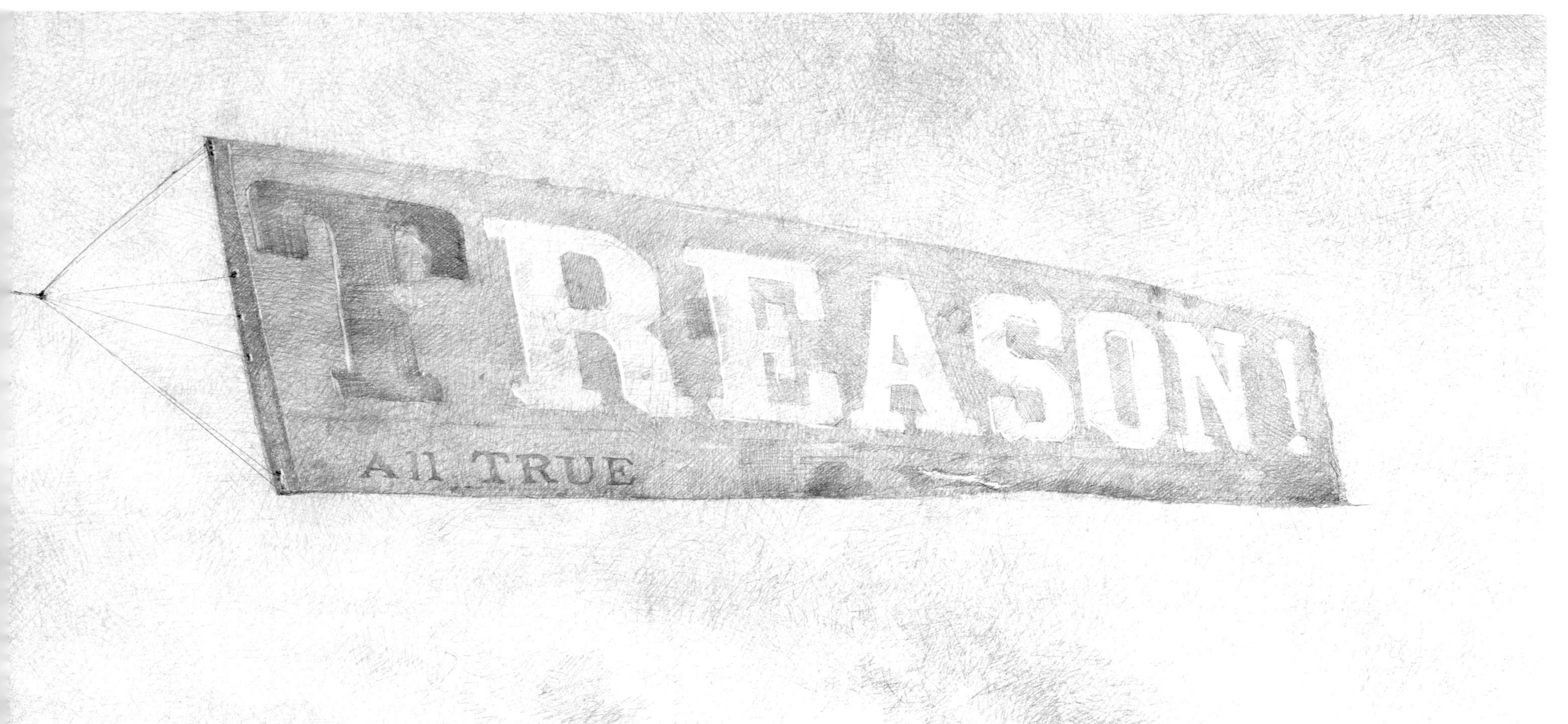
TREASON!
All TRUE

*Appleseed*

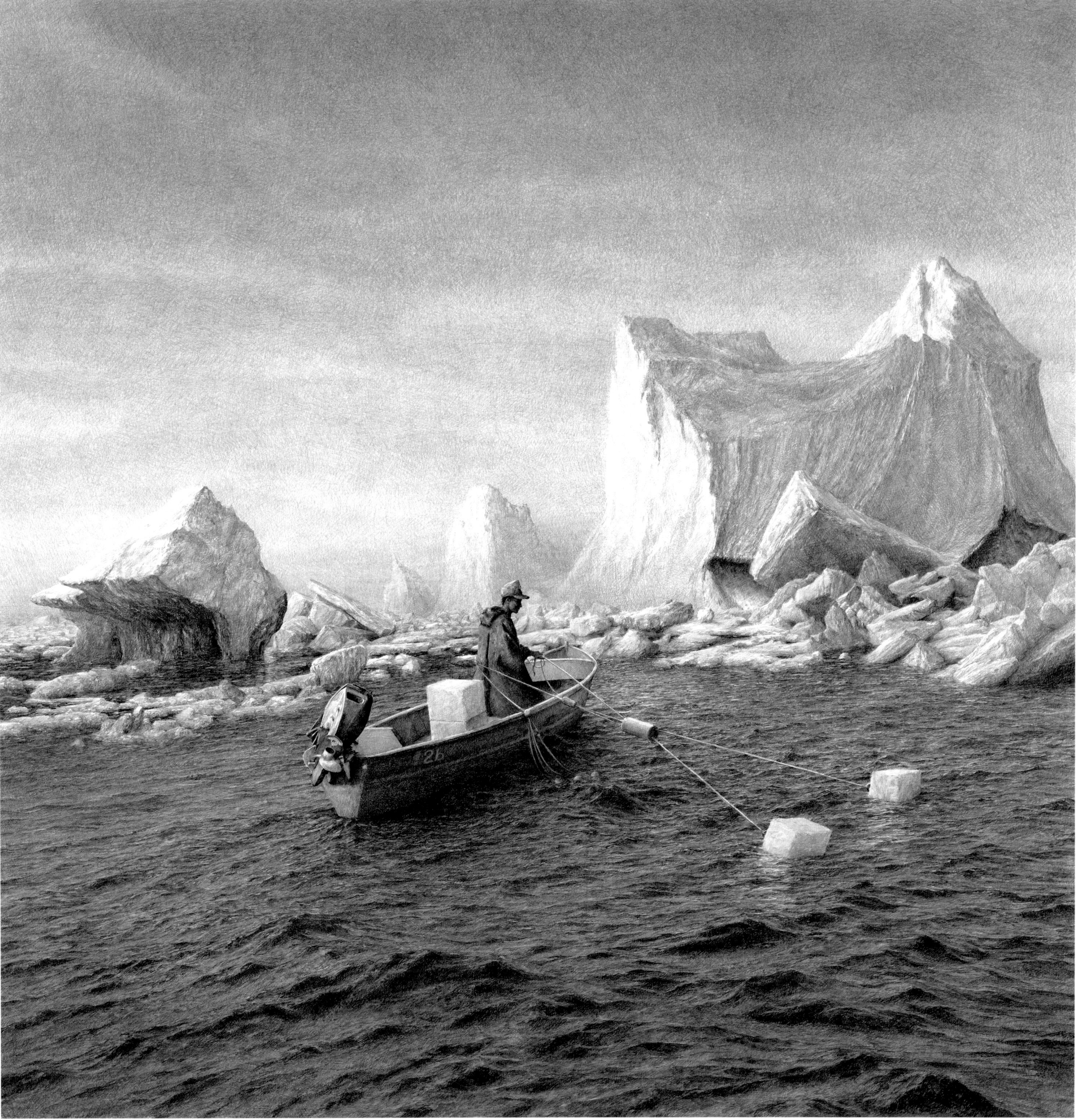
26

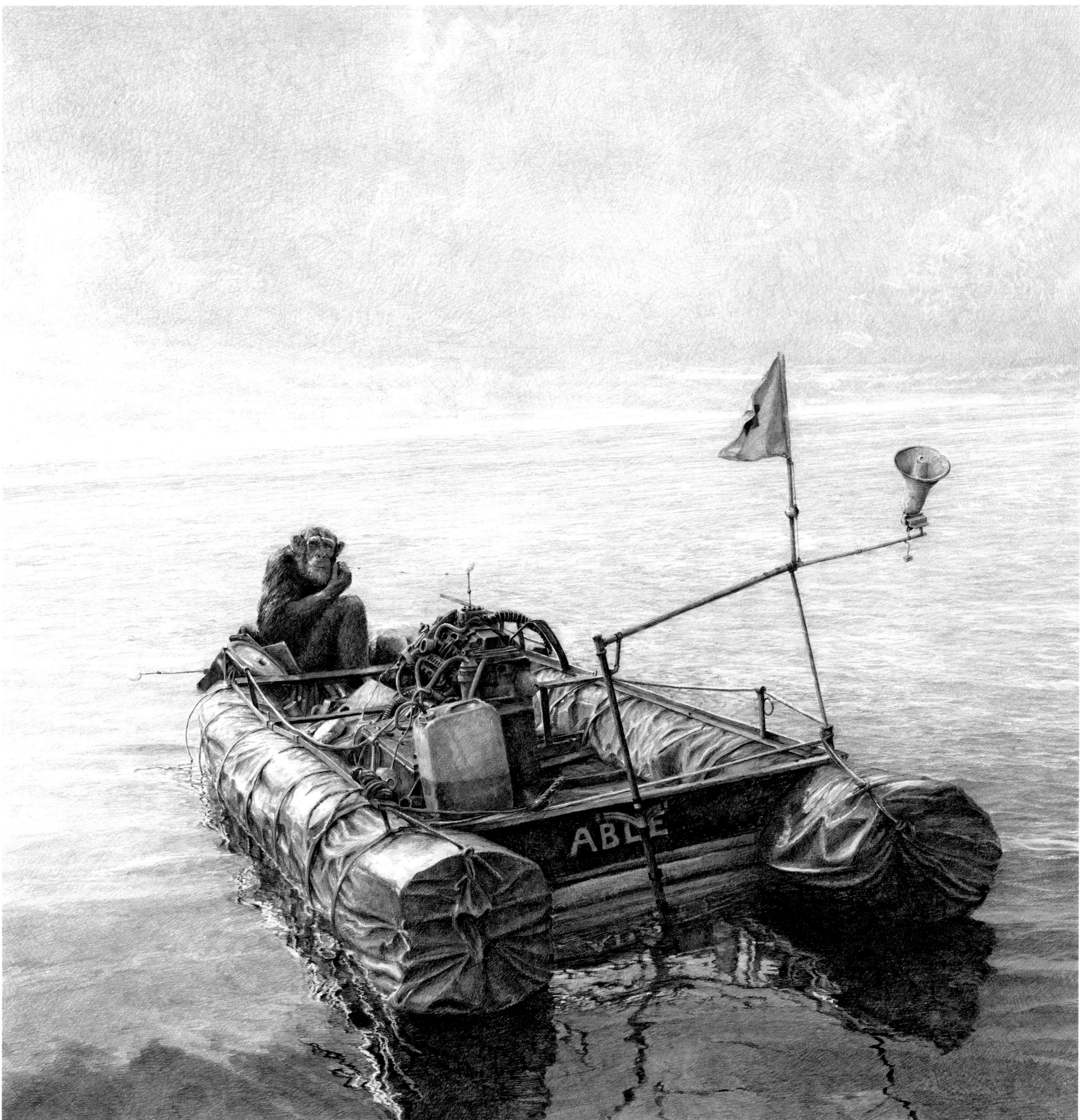
ABLE

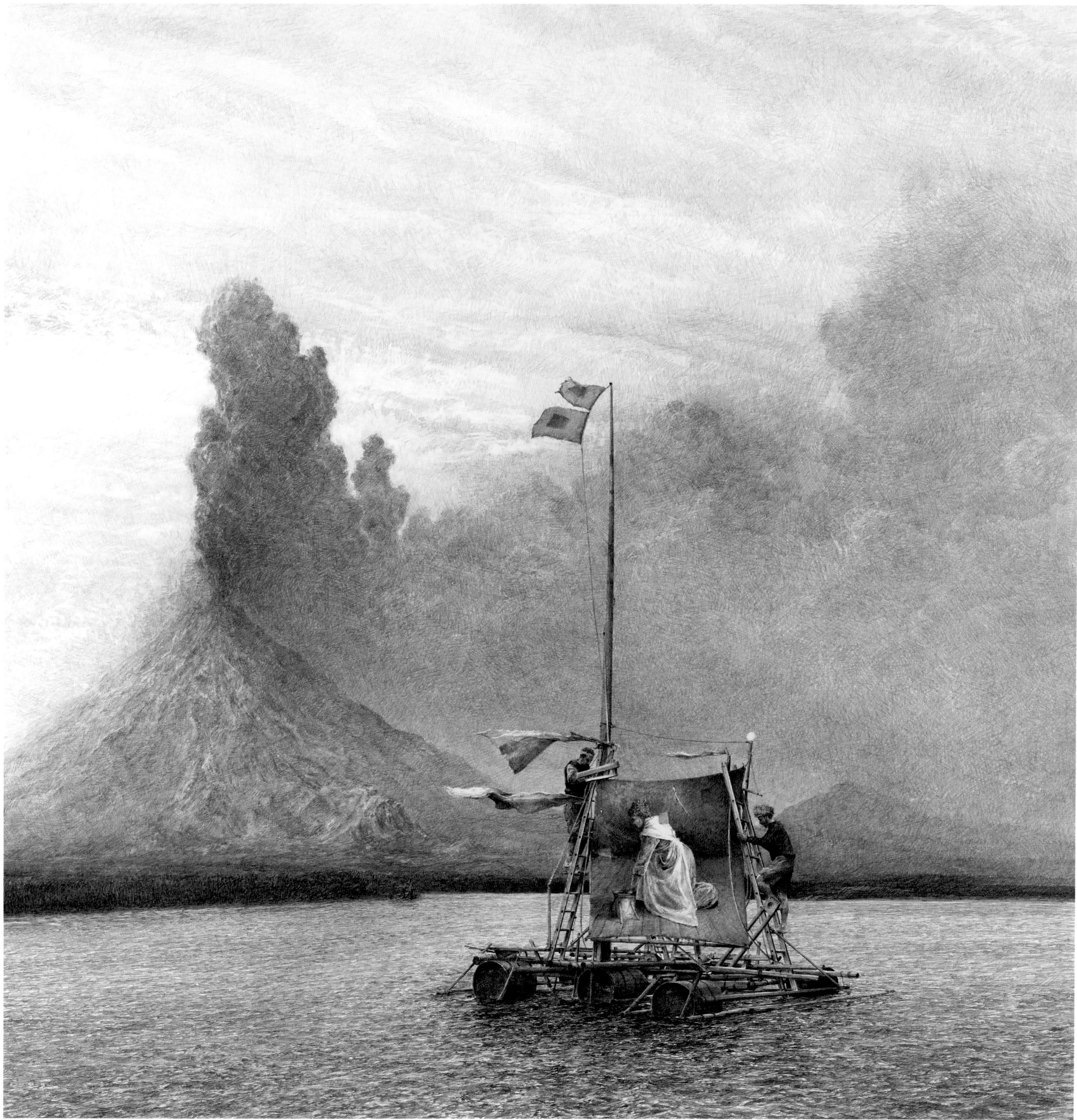

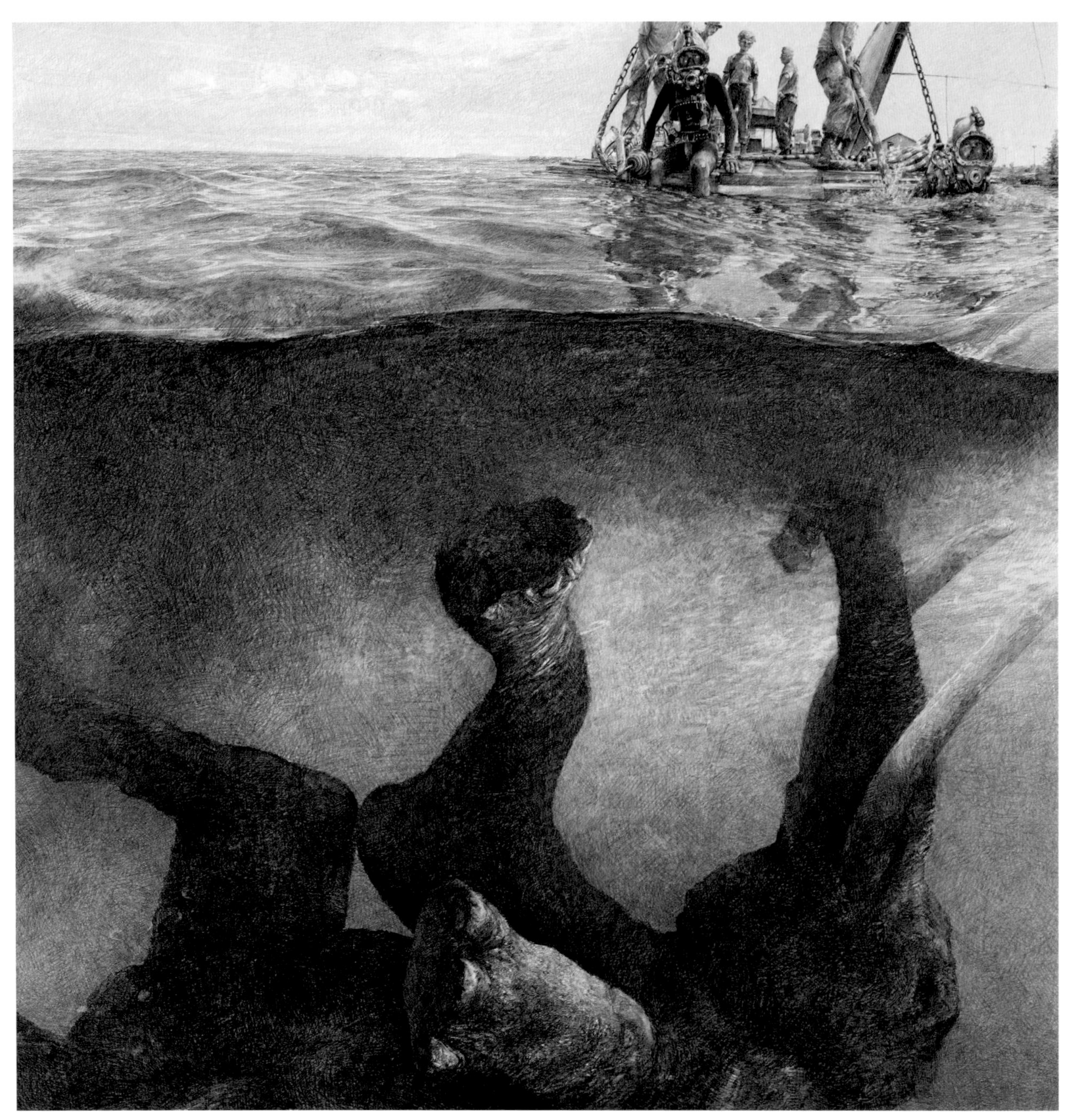

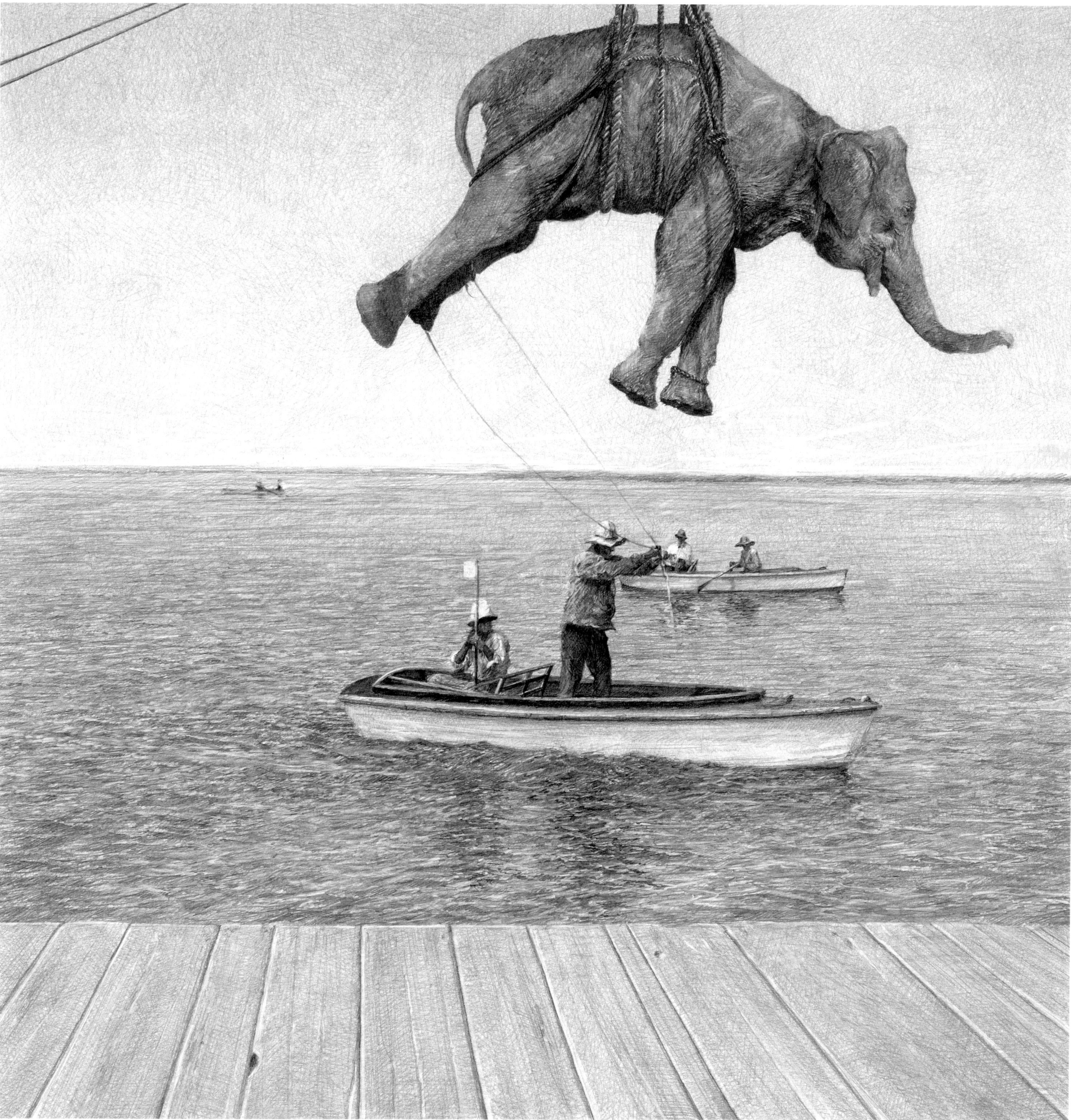

Previous pages:
*The Old Aristocratic Colors Breaking Through*
*Influx*

*State of Alaska*

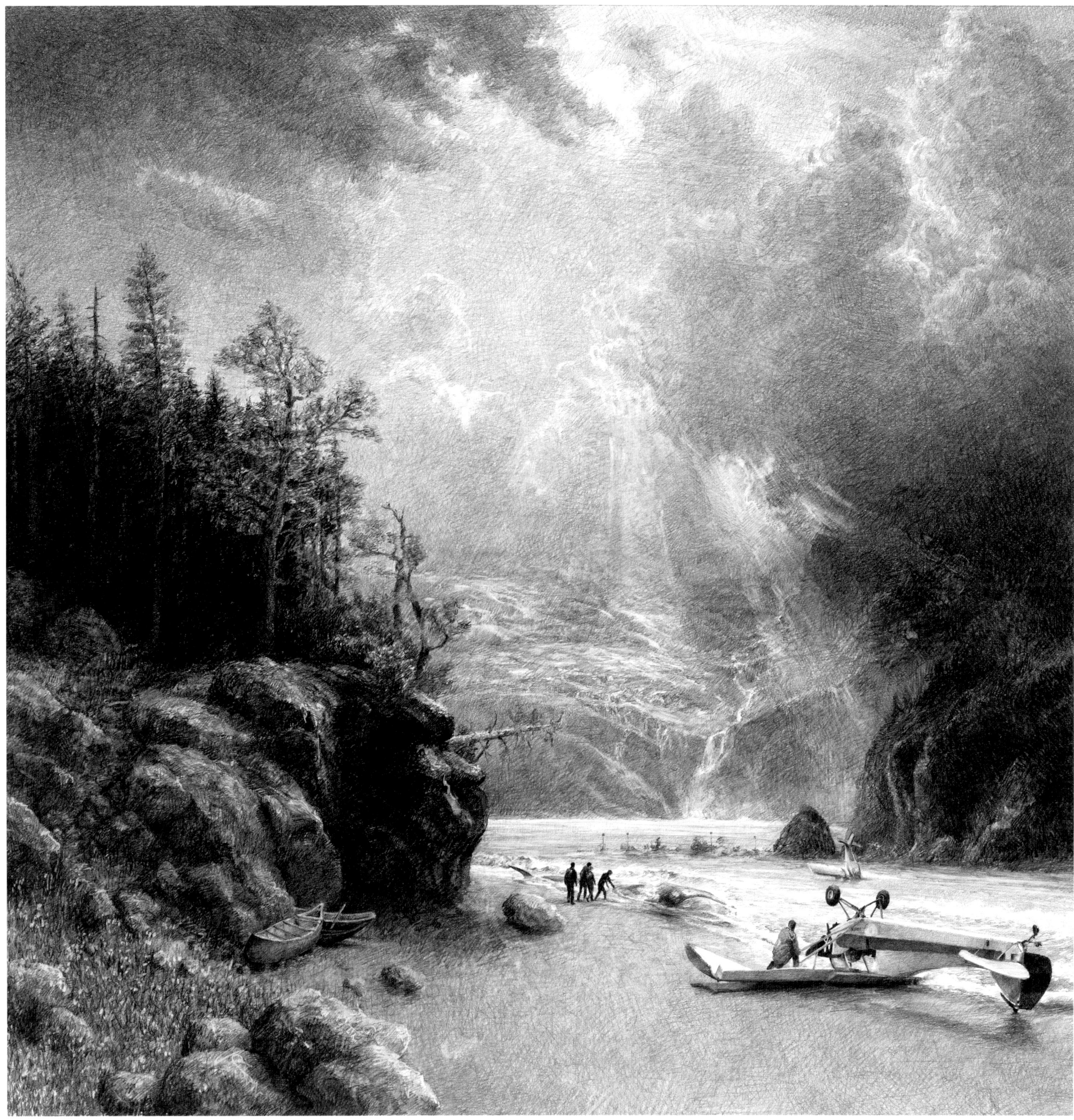

*Moby Dick*

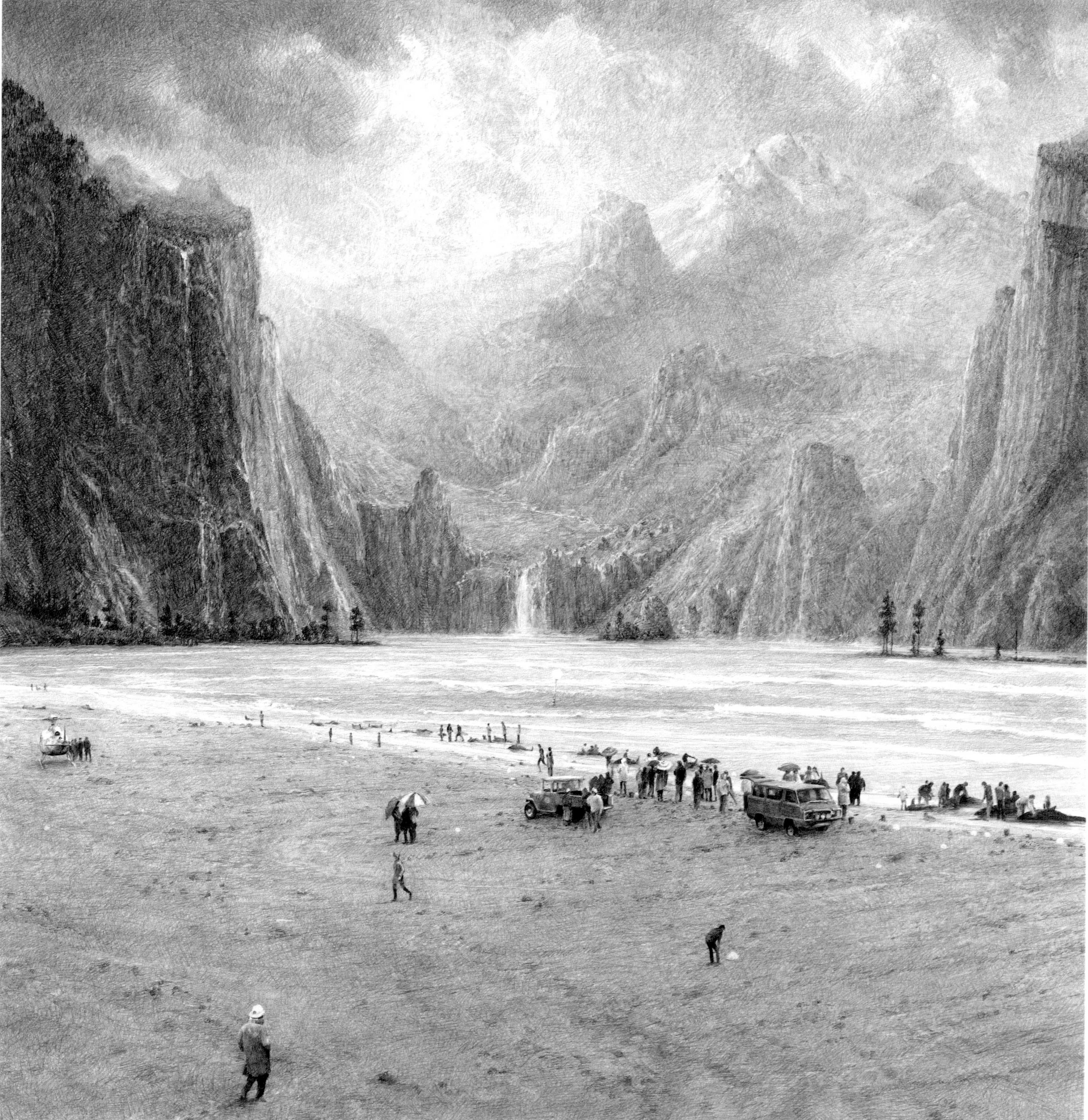

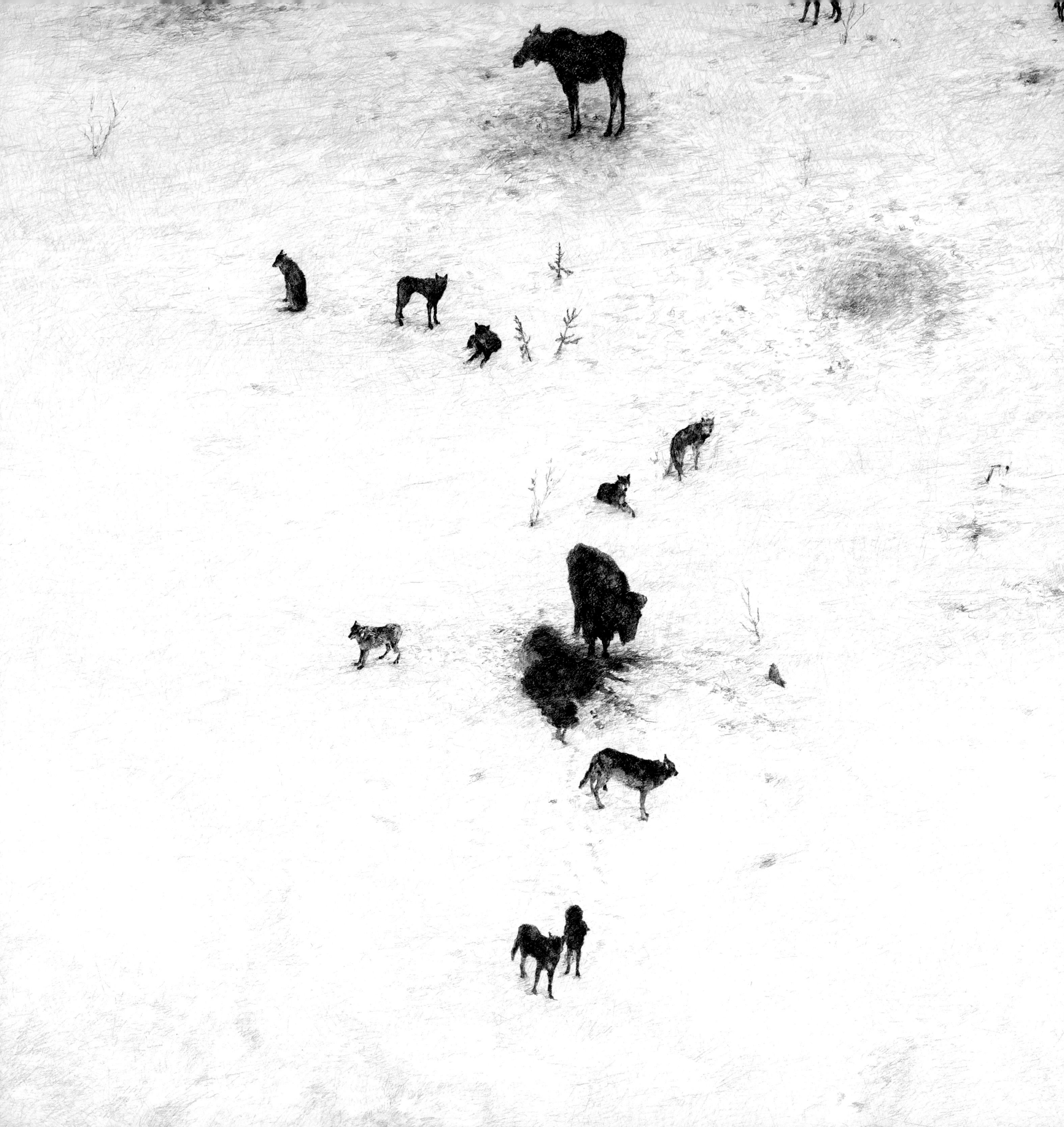

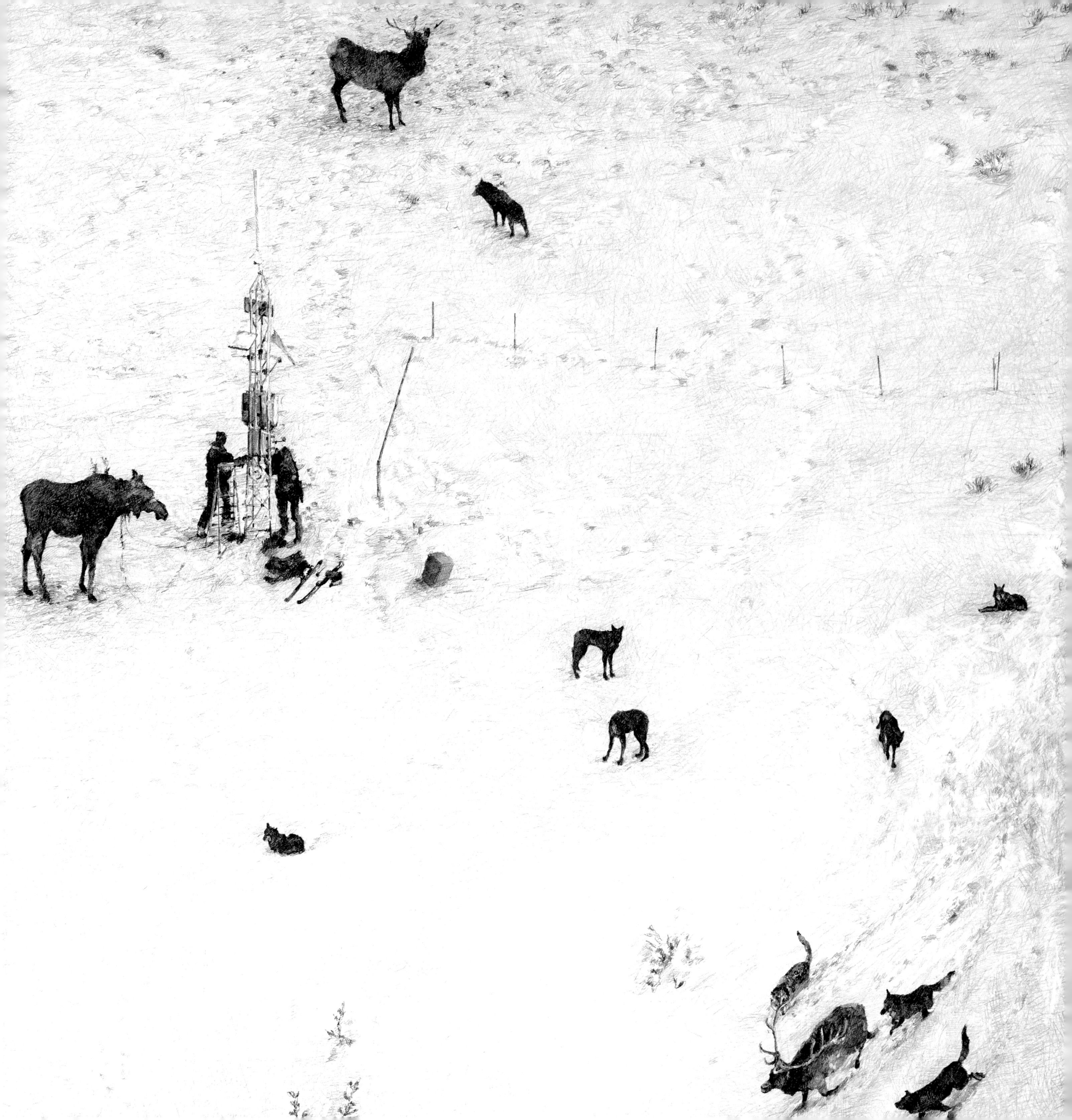

Previous pages:
*Albert Bierstadt*, detail

*Fiefdom*

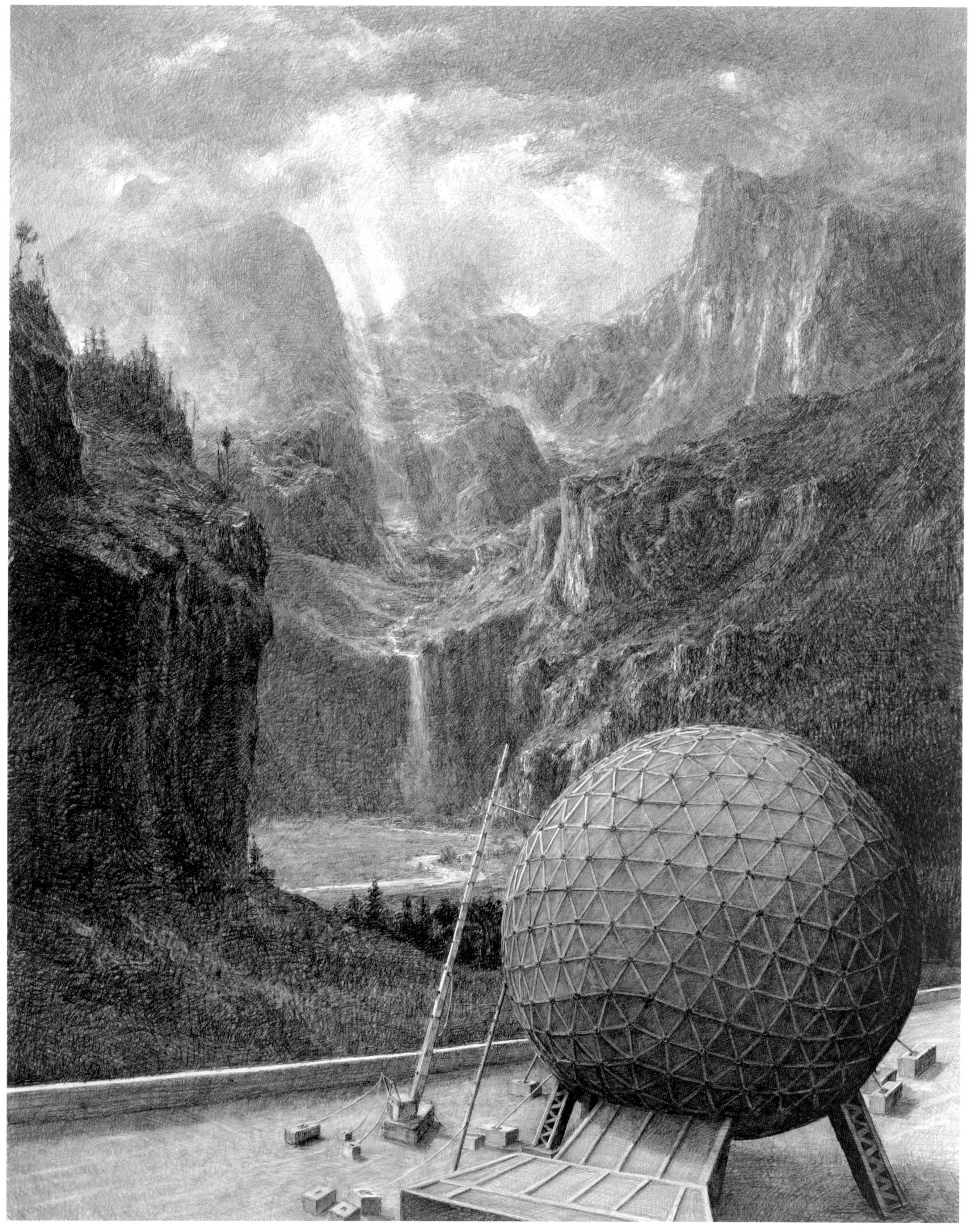

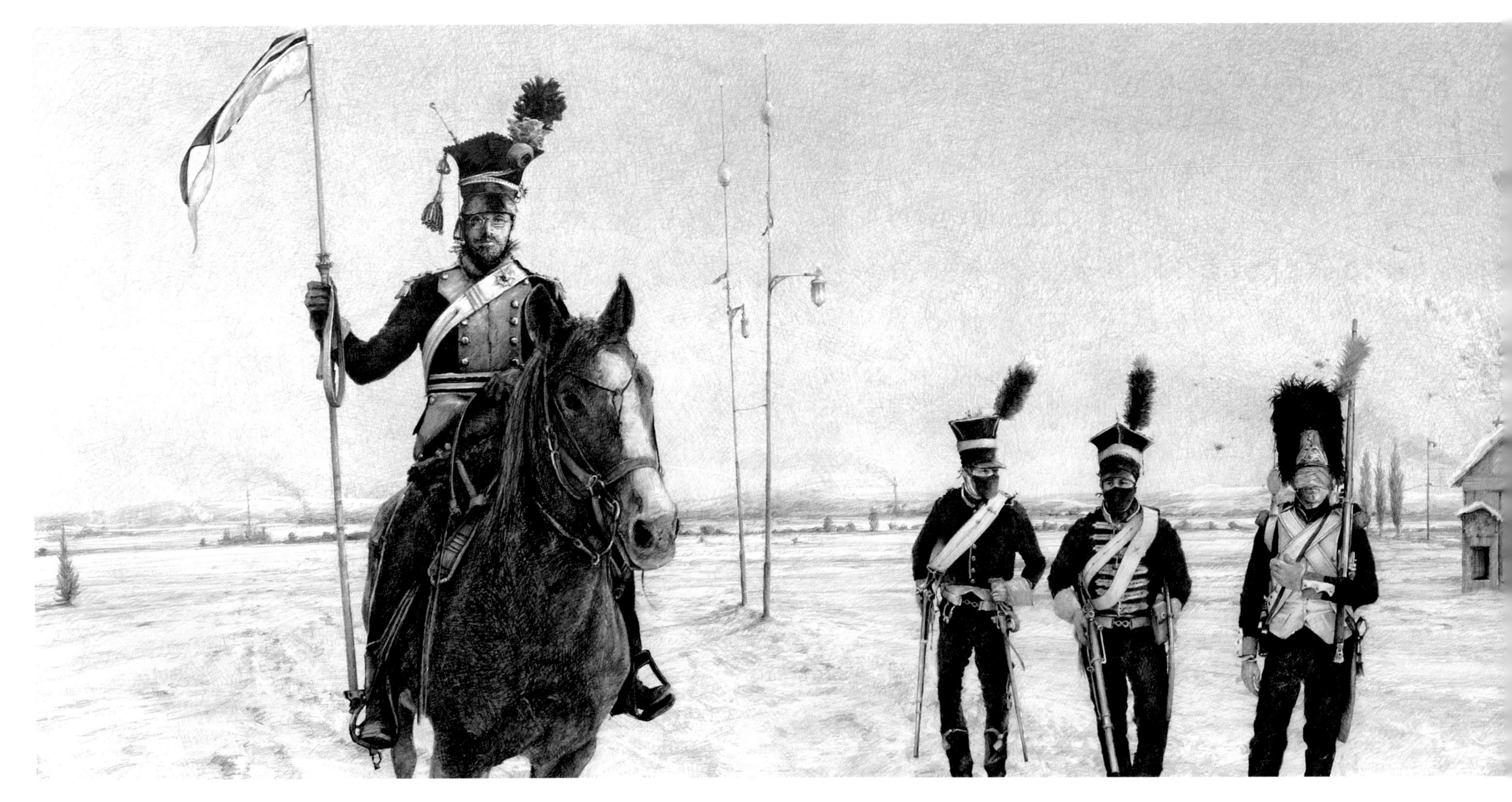

*Napoleon Custer Mithradetes of Whitehall*

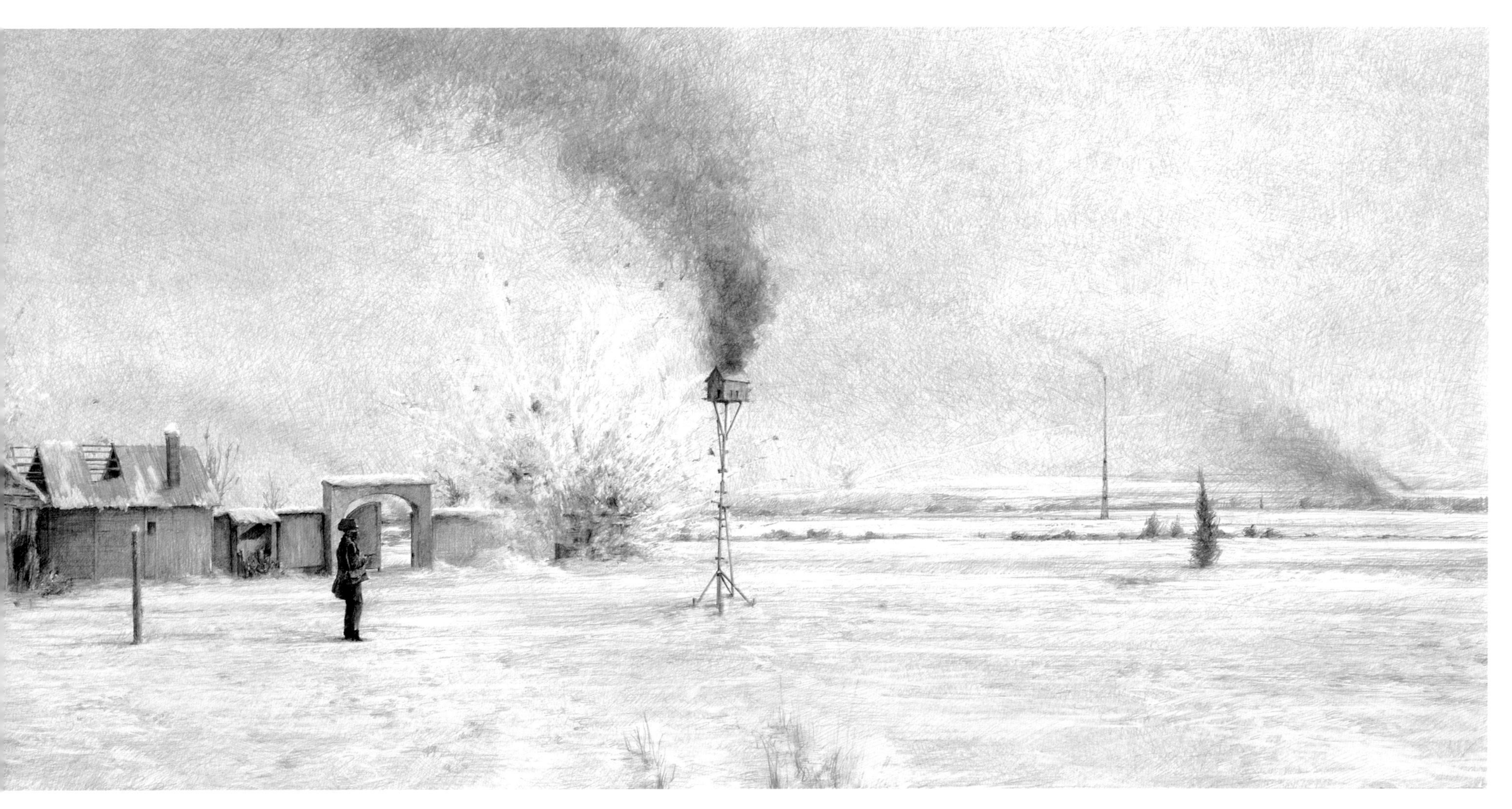

*Nueva Iguarán*

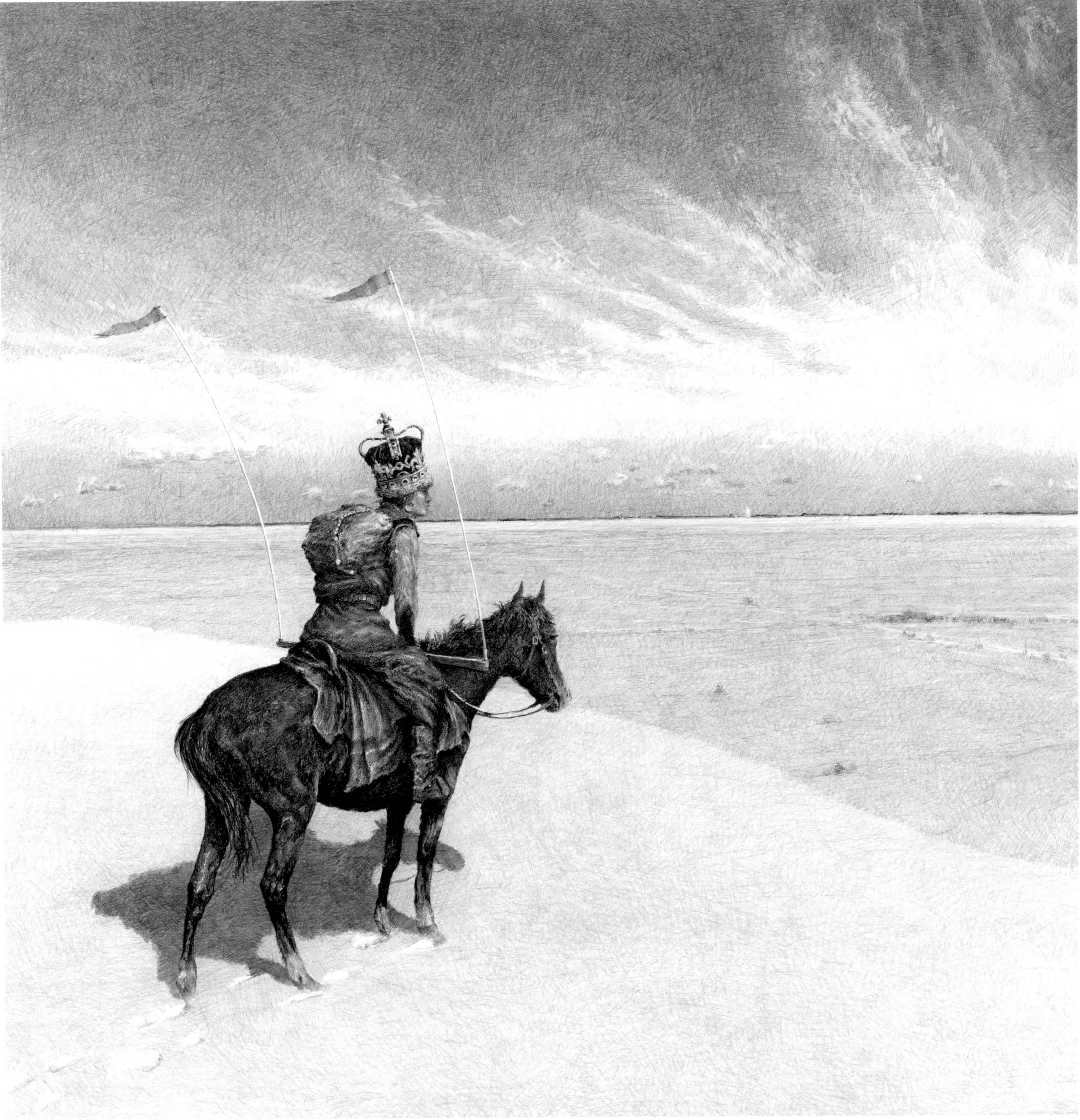

*Water Guard*

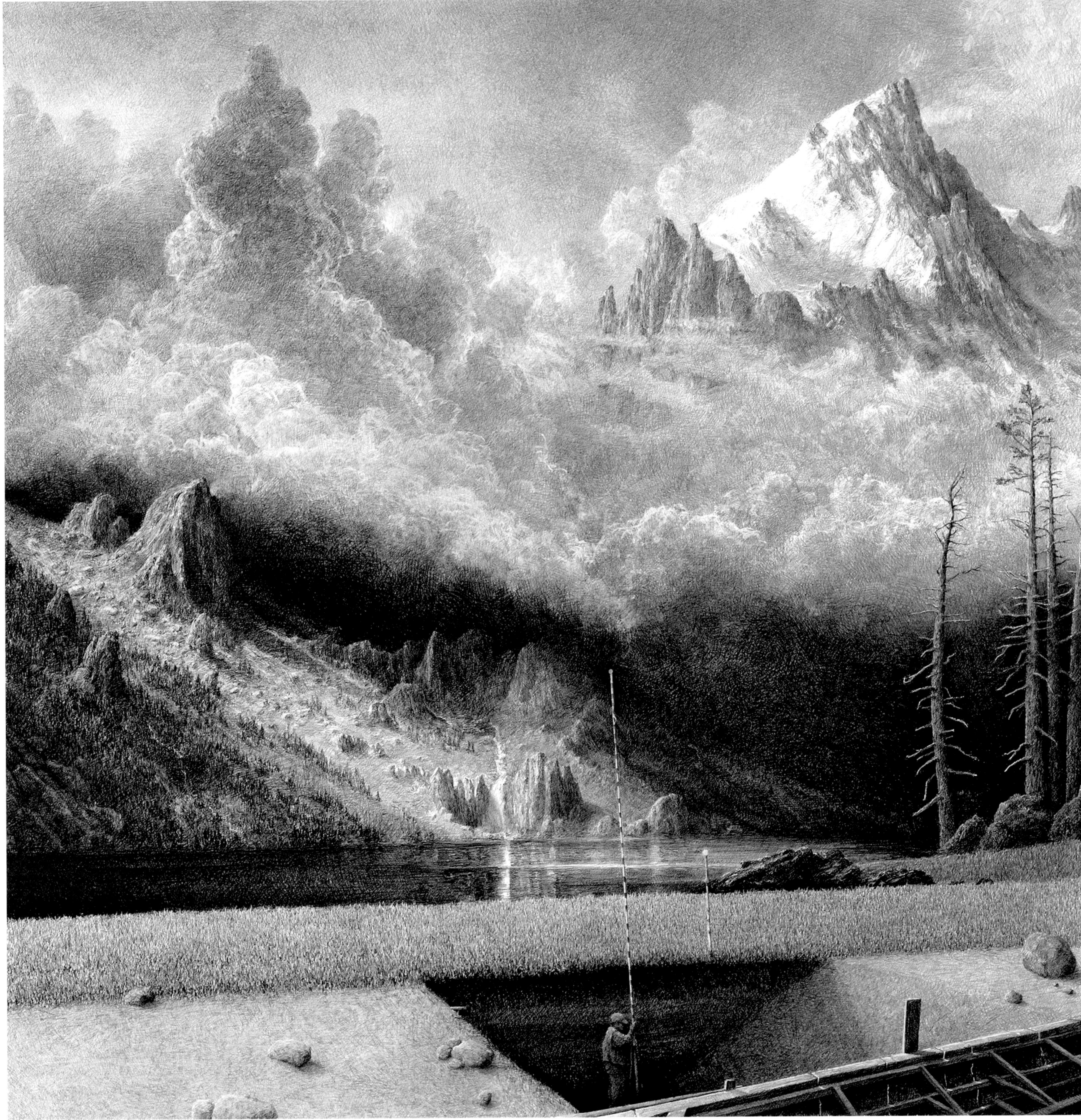

*Expansion*

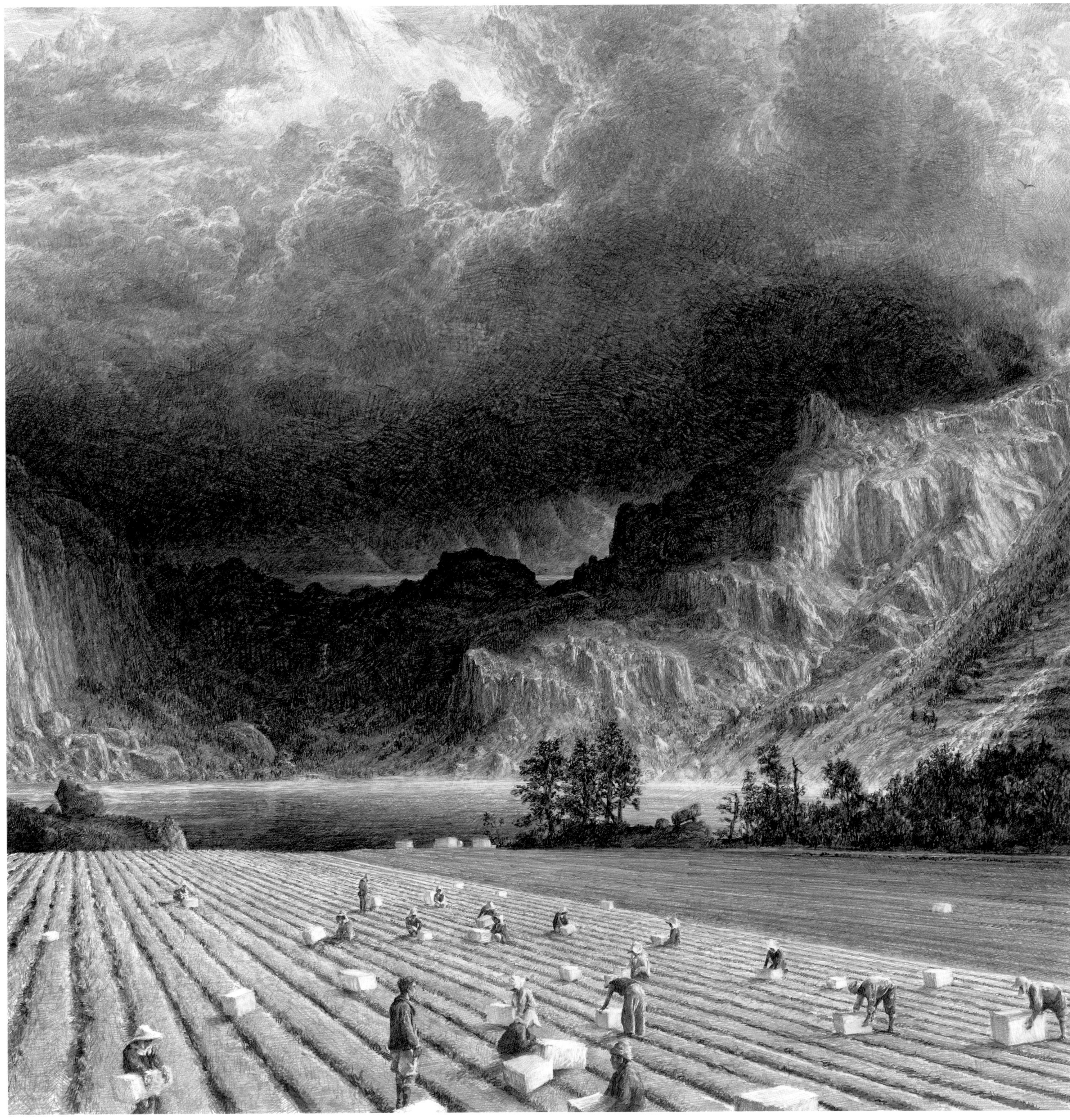

*Ellesmere Island Tar Pit*

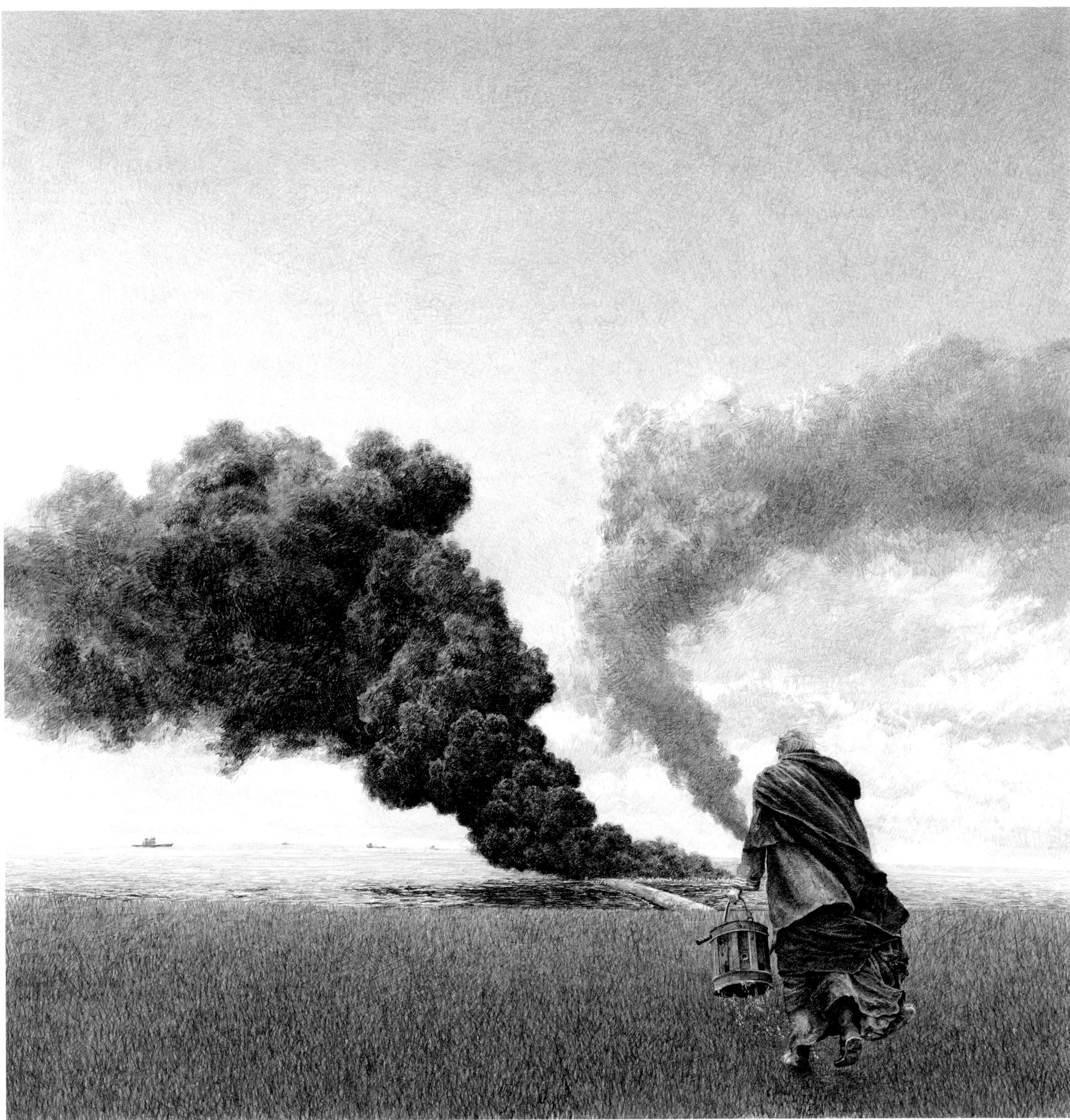

State of Massachusetts

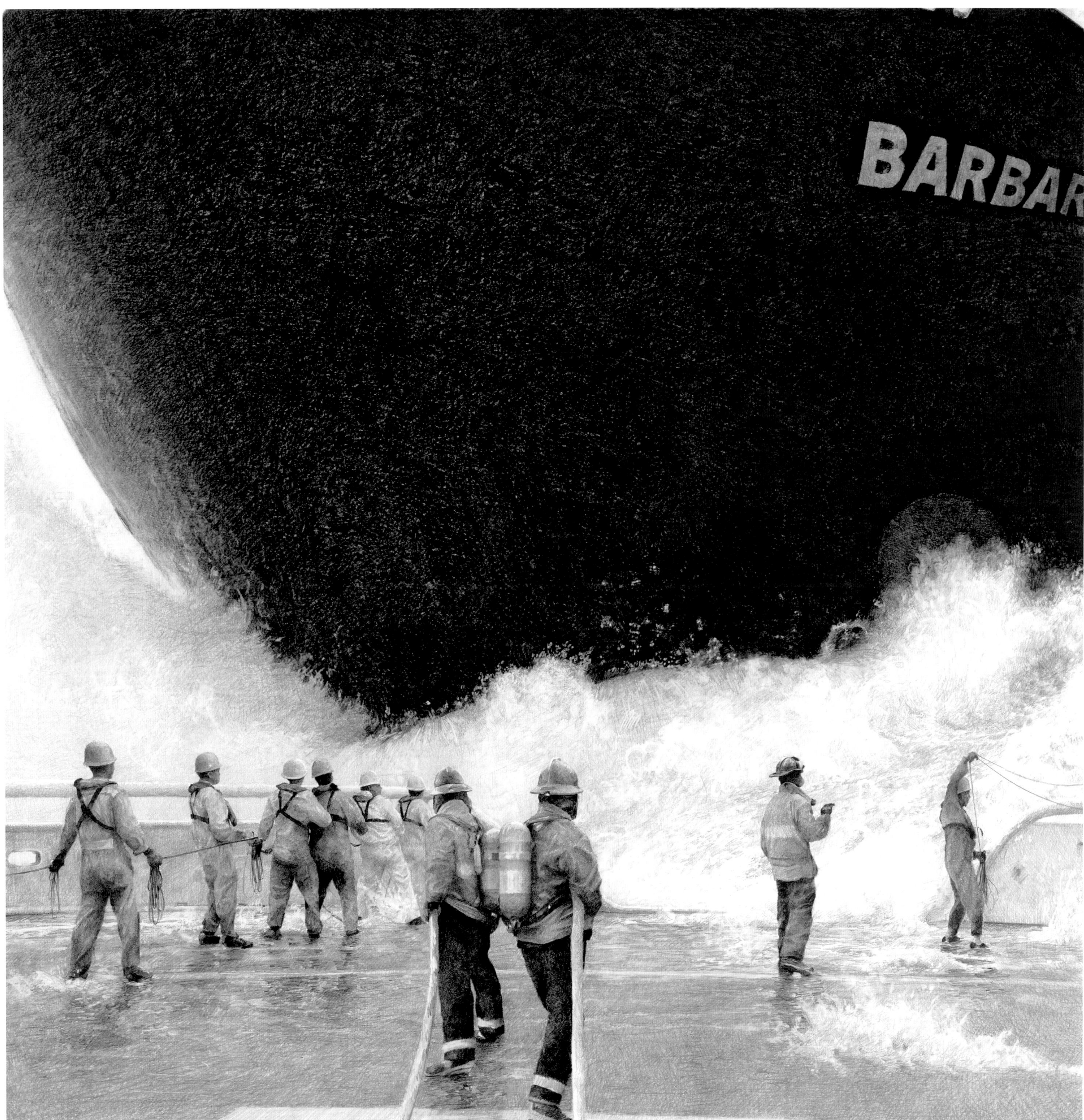
BARBAR

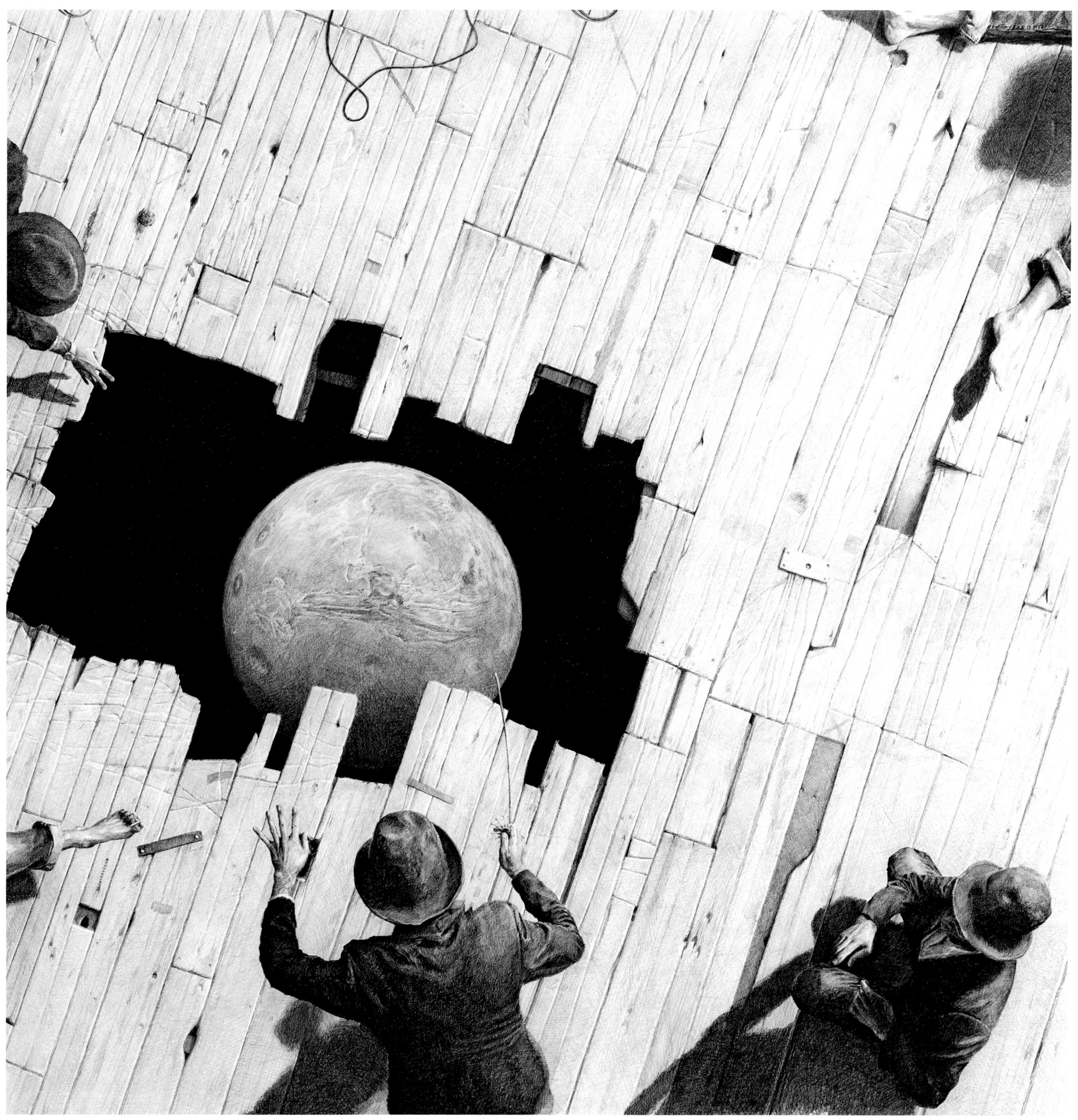

# Prosceniums

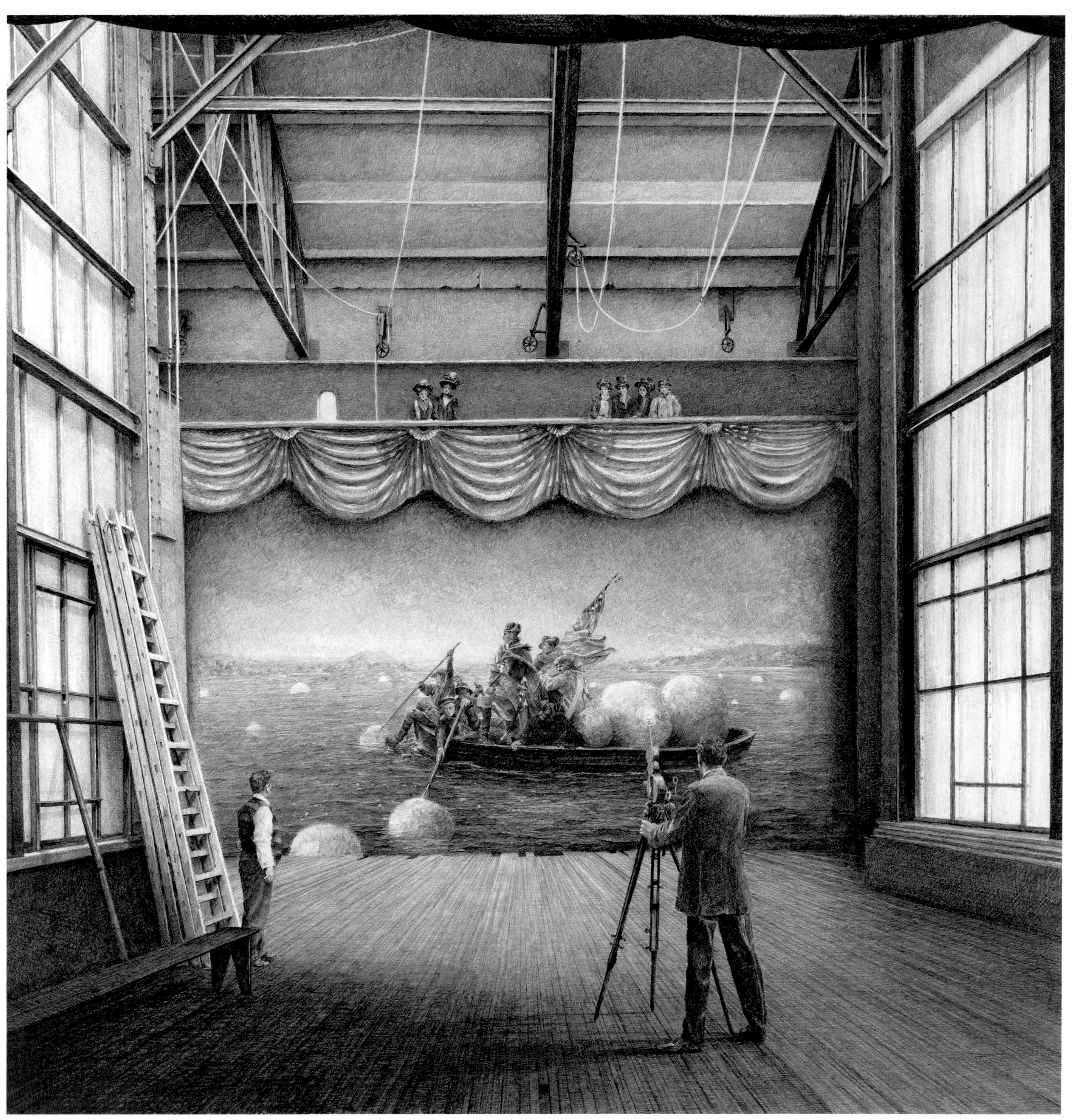

Previous page:
*Captains of Revision*

*State of Nevada*

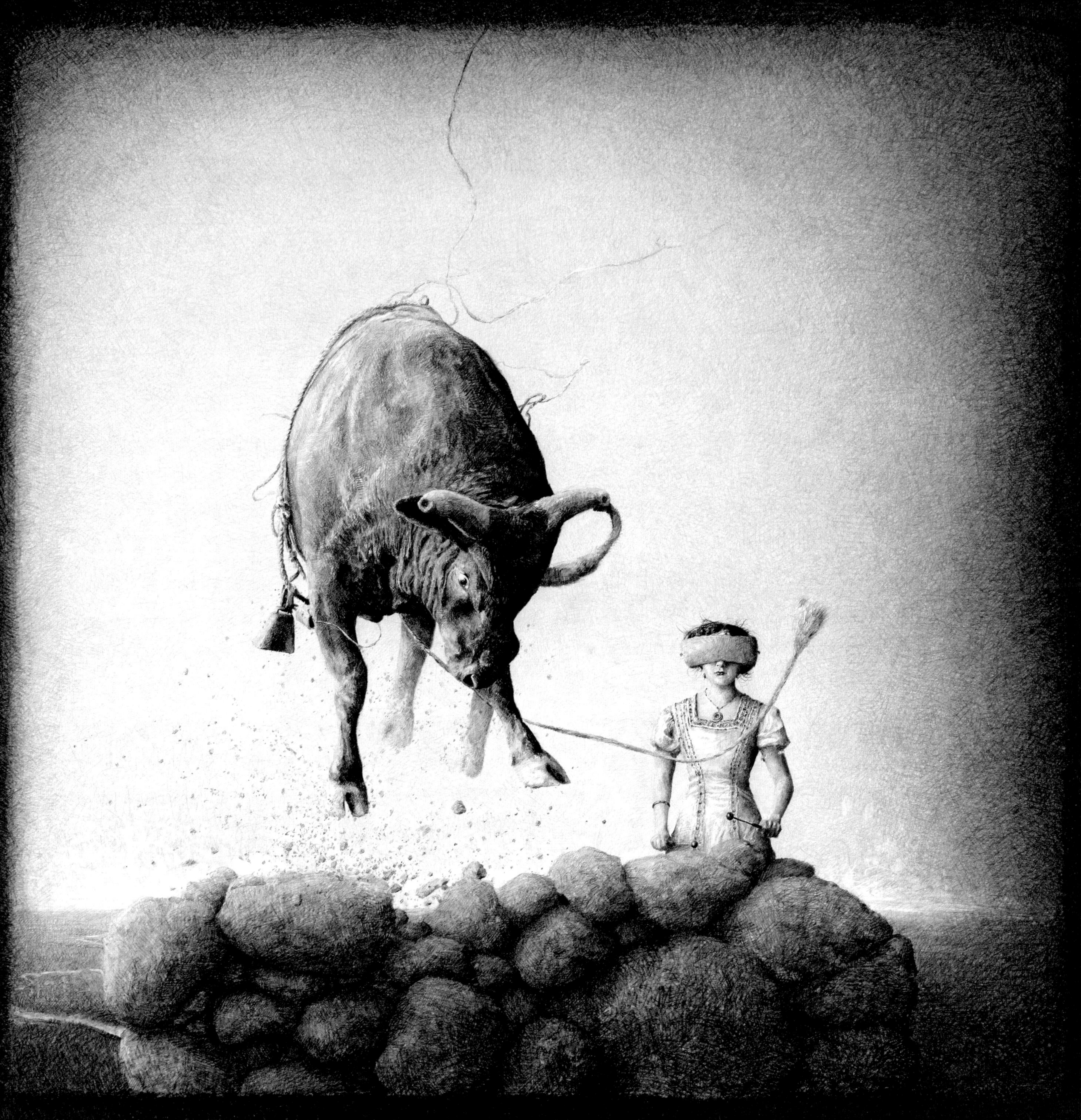

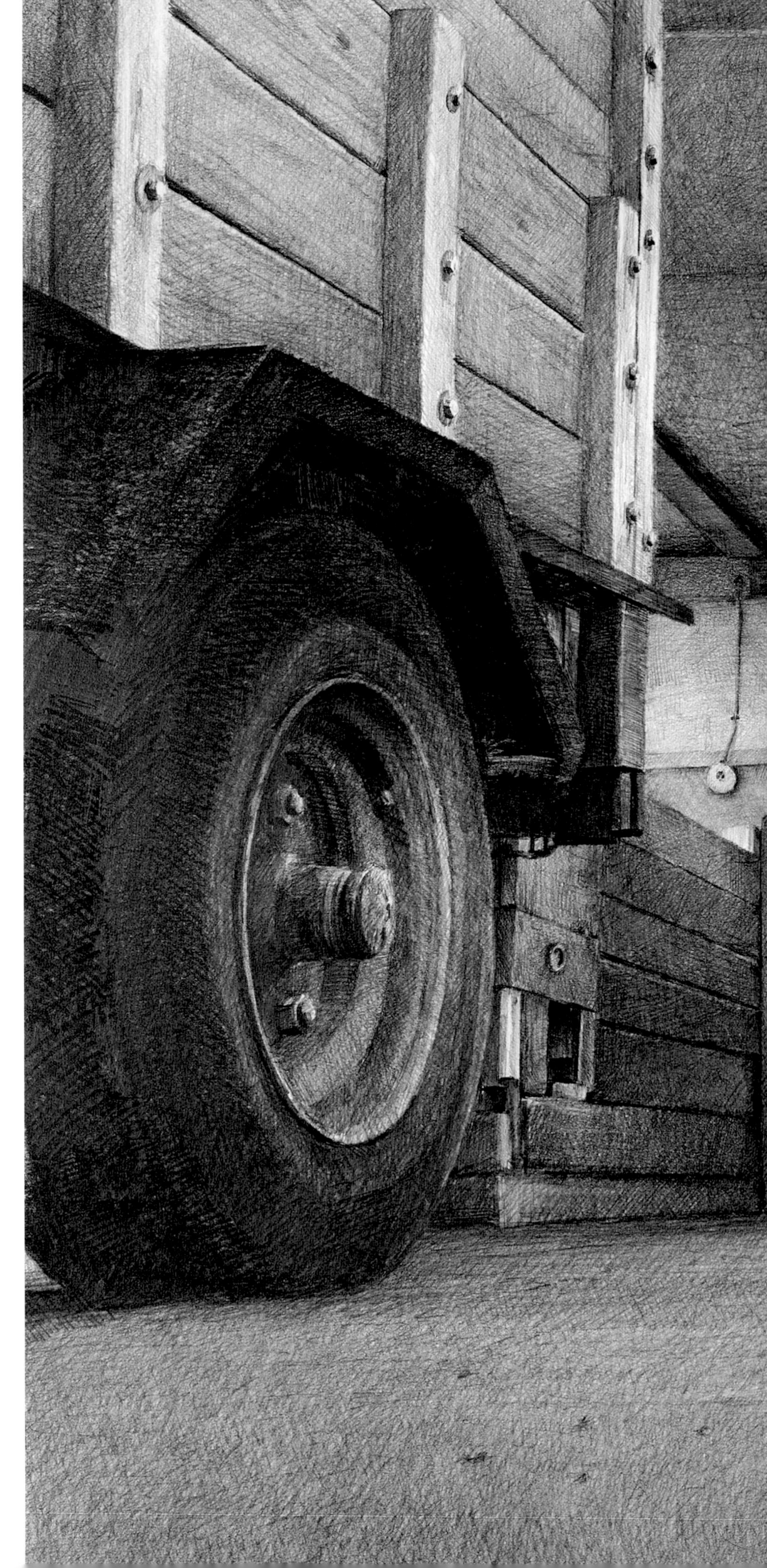

*Alibi*, detail

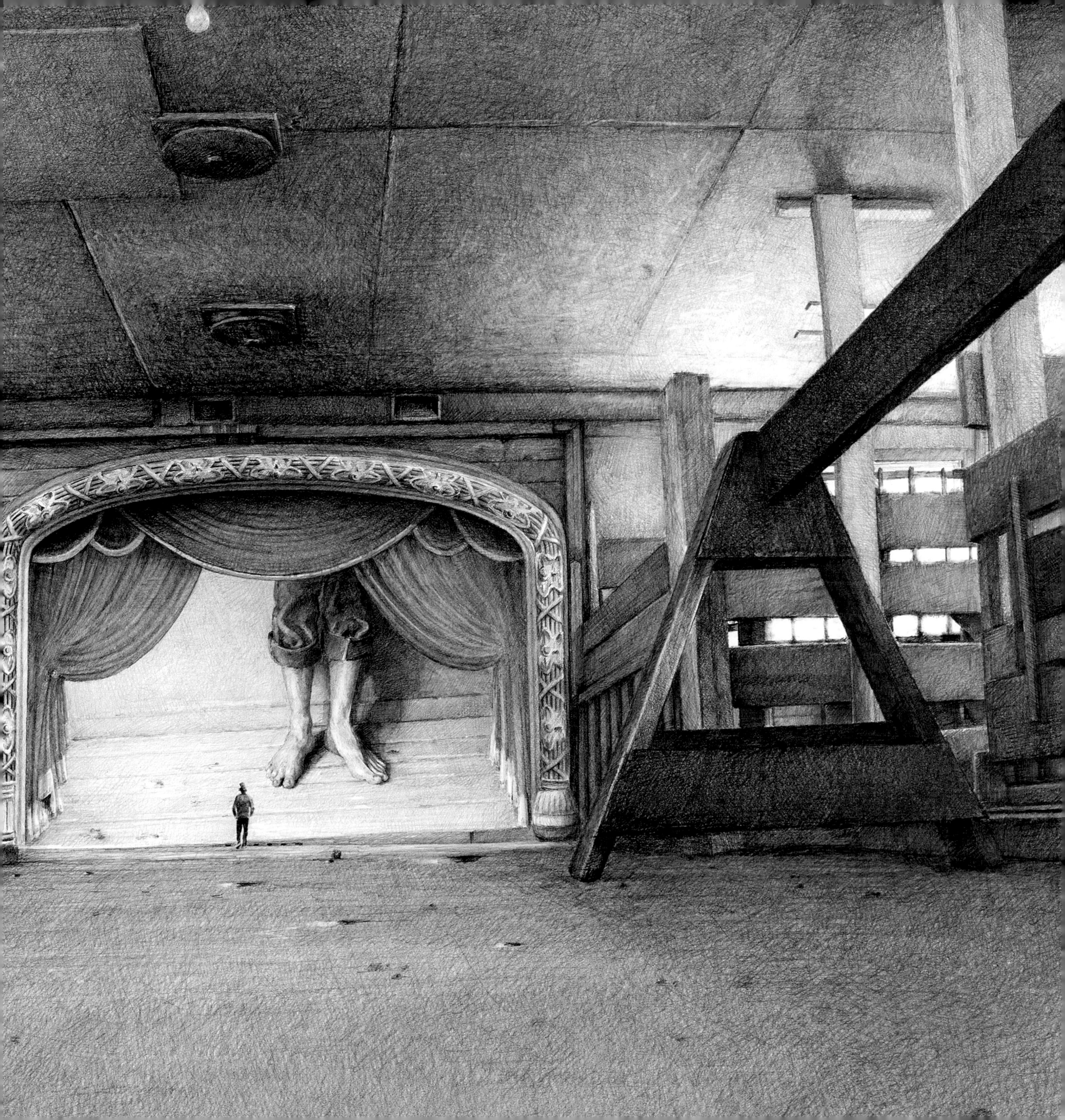

State of Texas

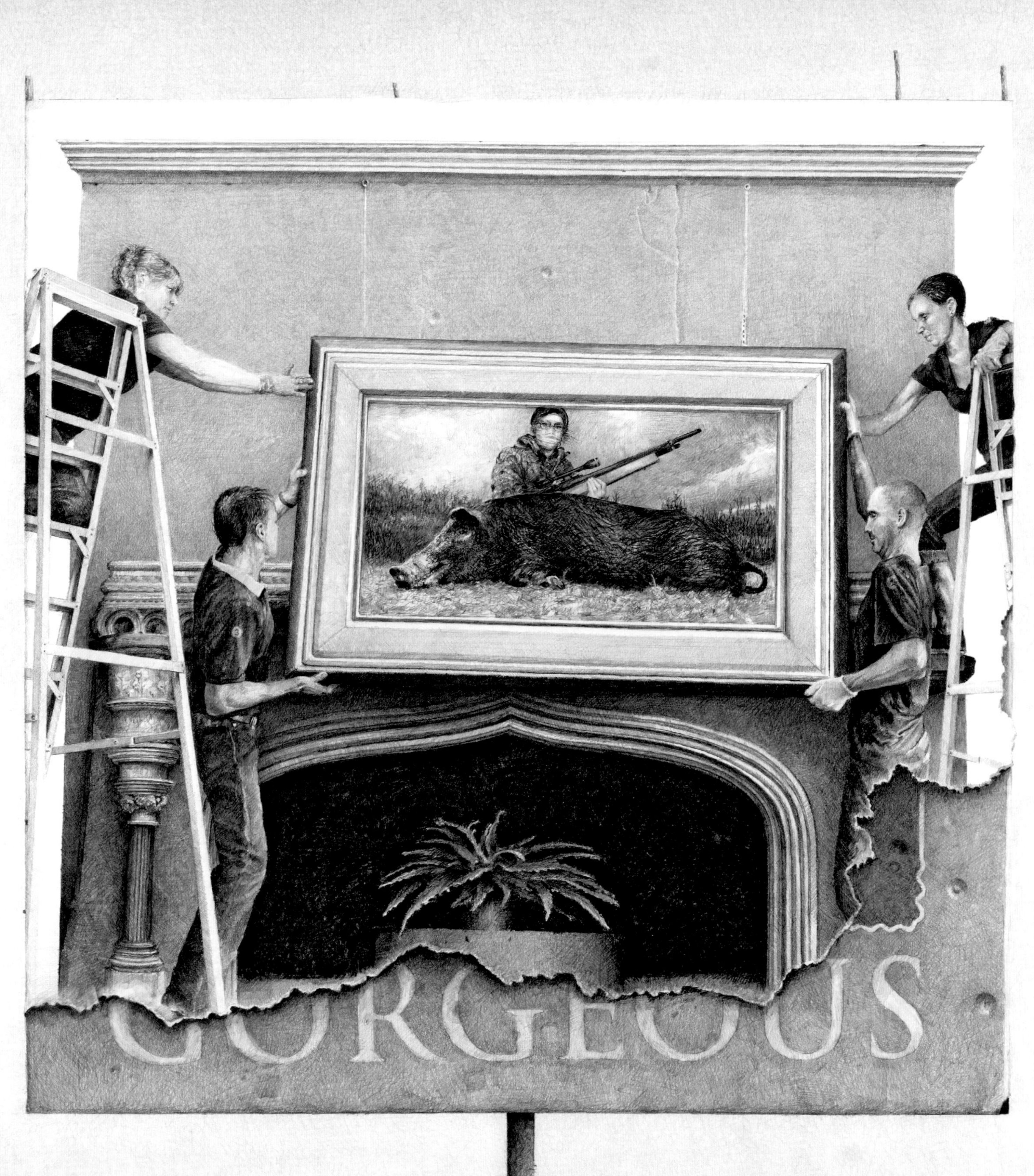
GORGEOUS

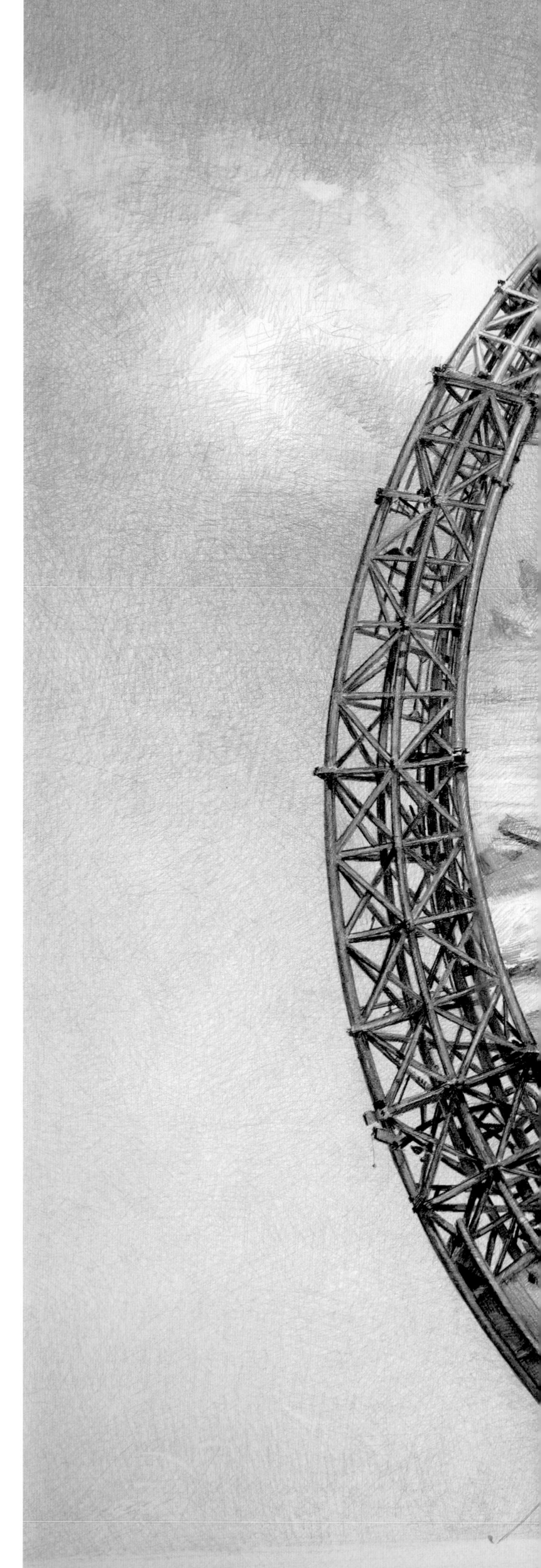

*Agitprop*, detail

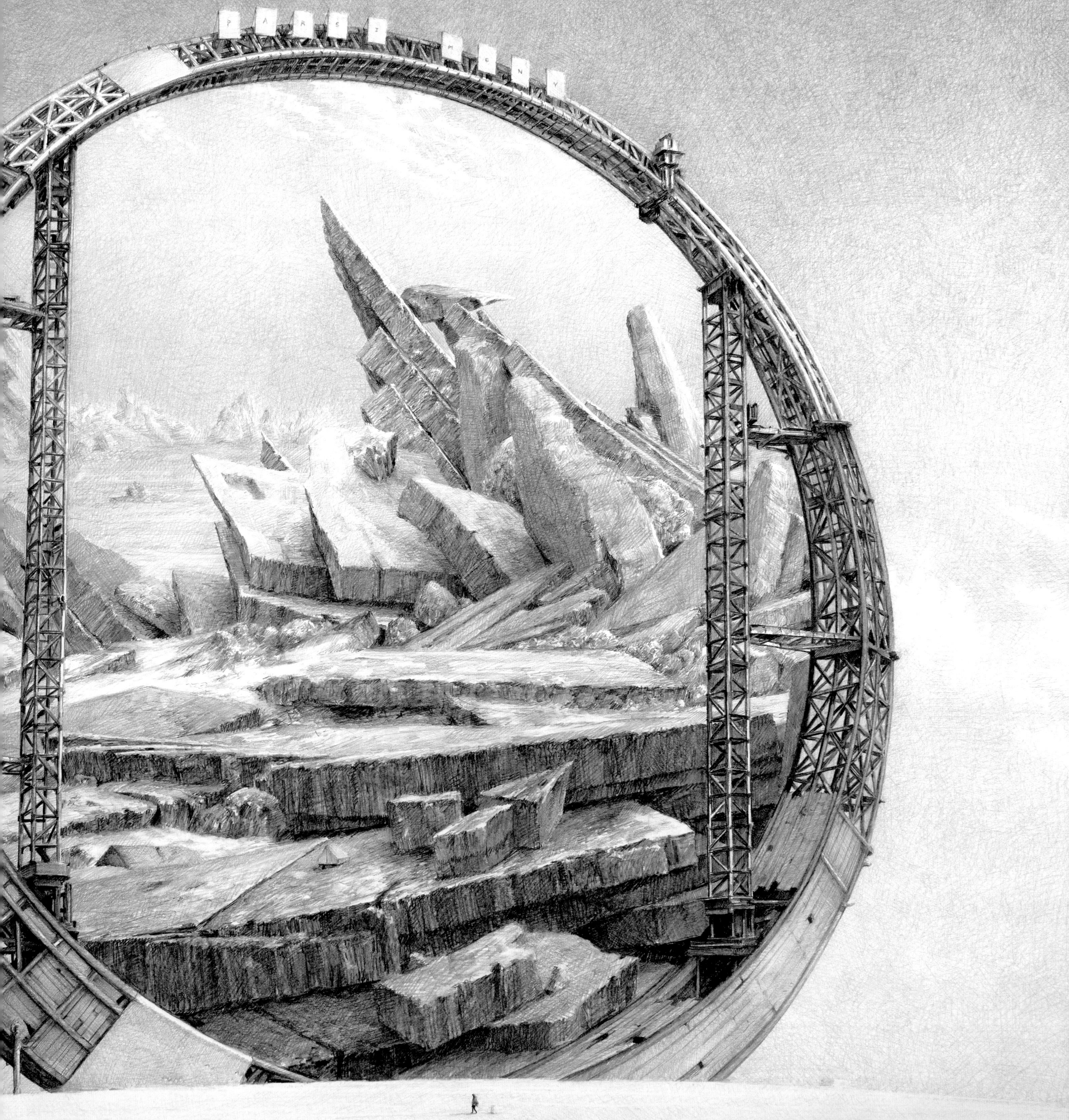
PARSIMONY

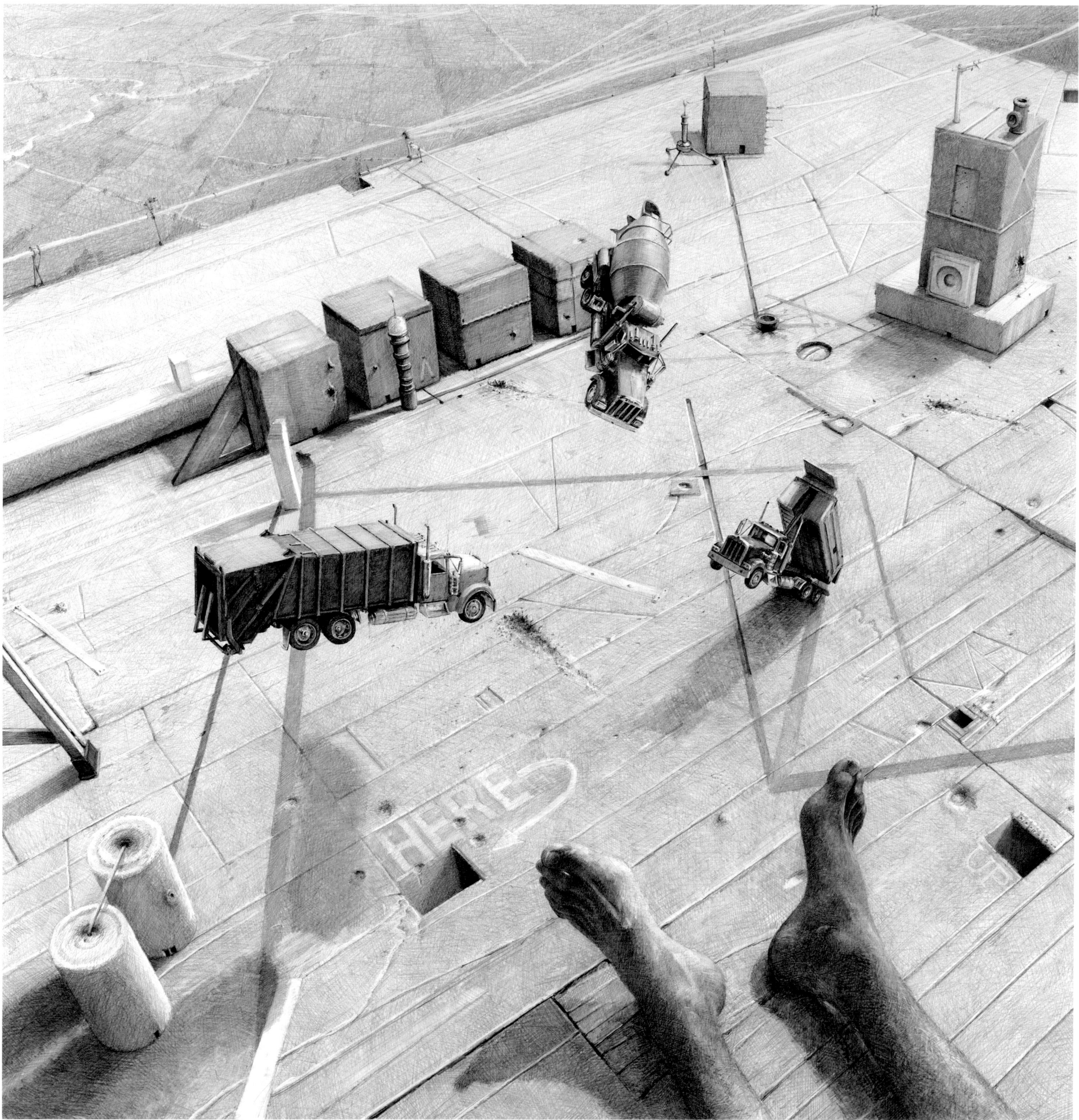
HERE
UP

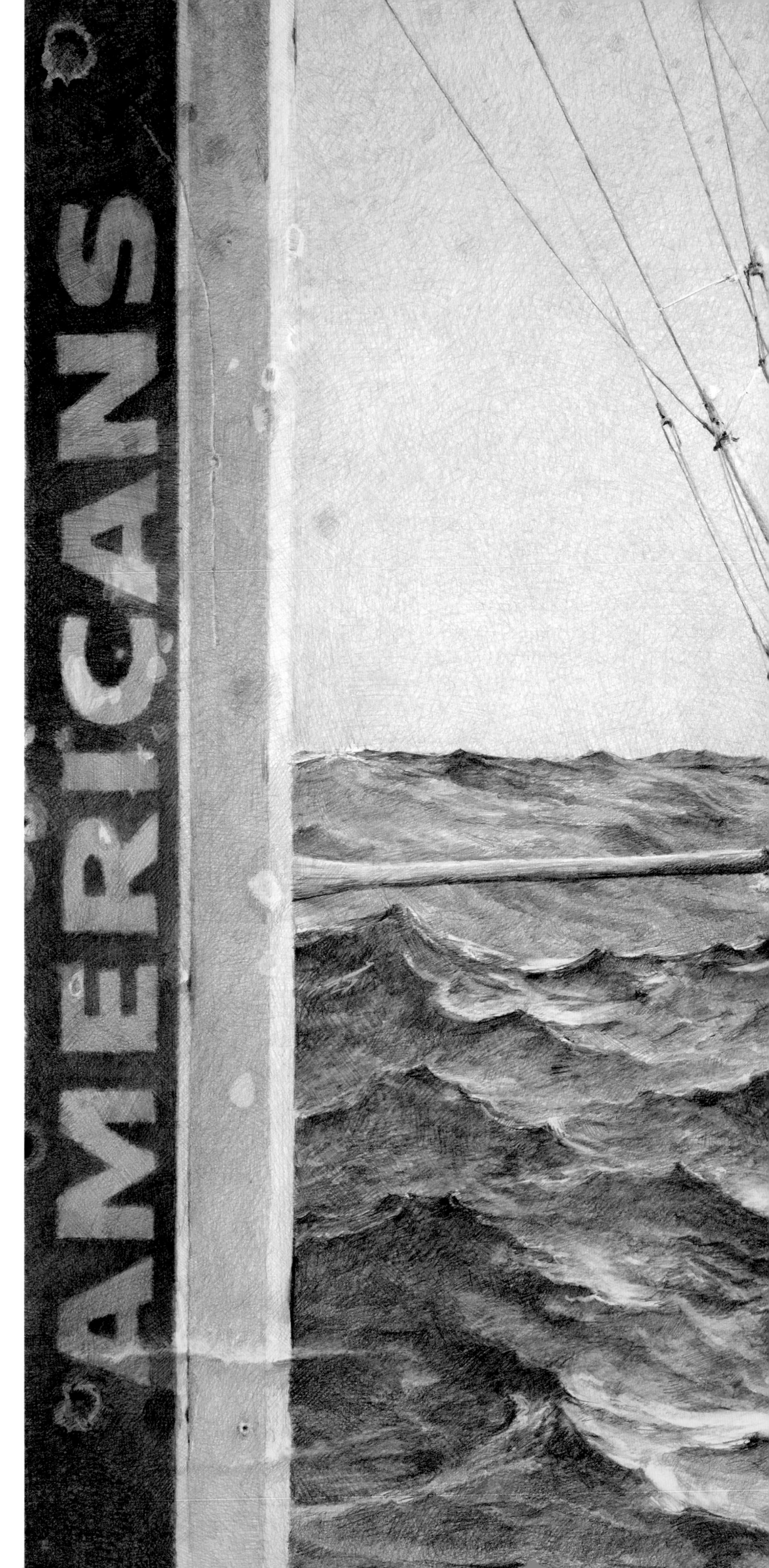


*Make No Parley*, detail

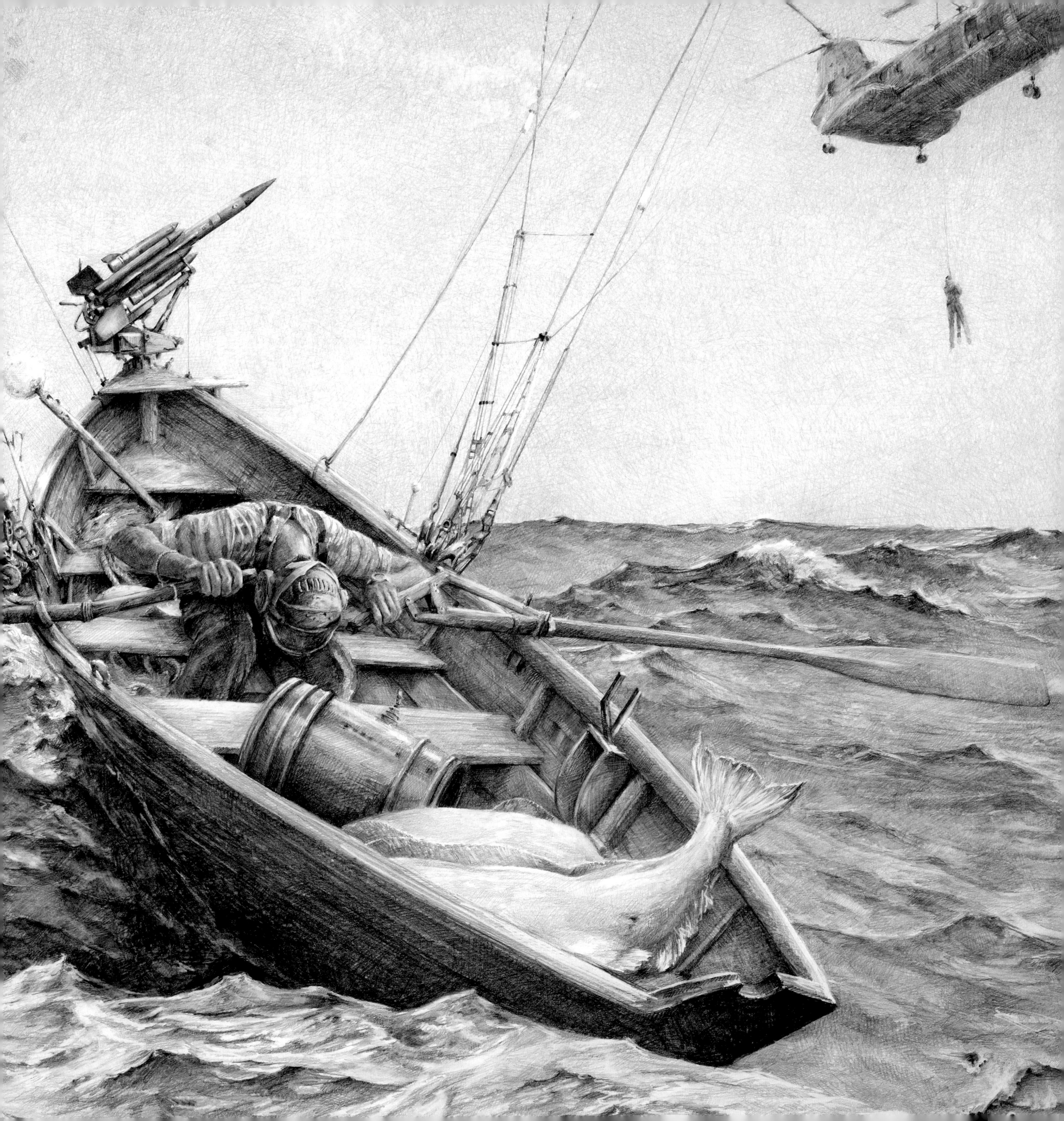

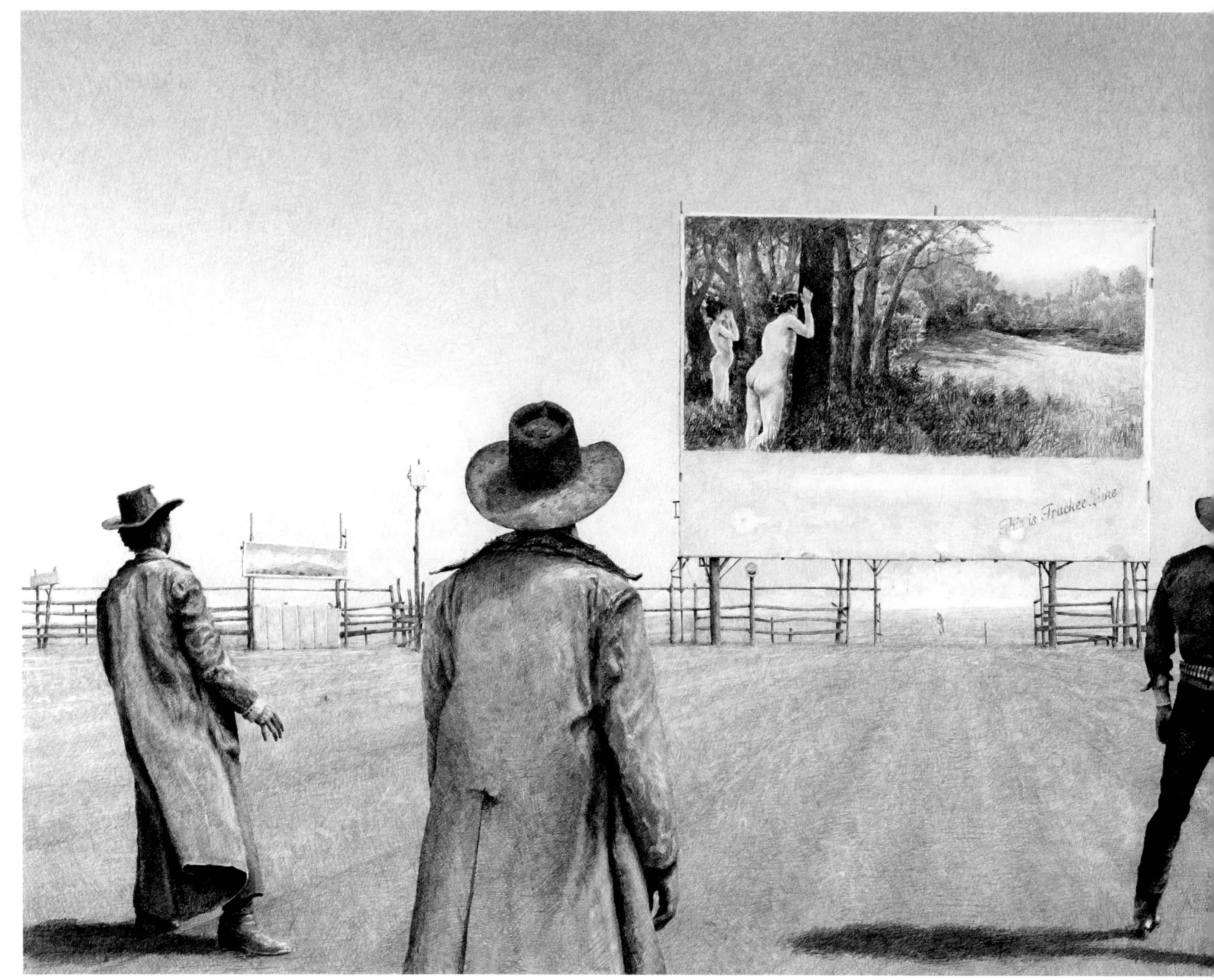


State of California

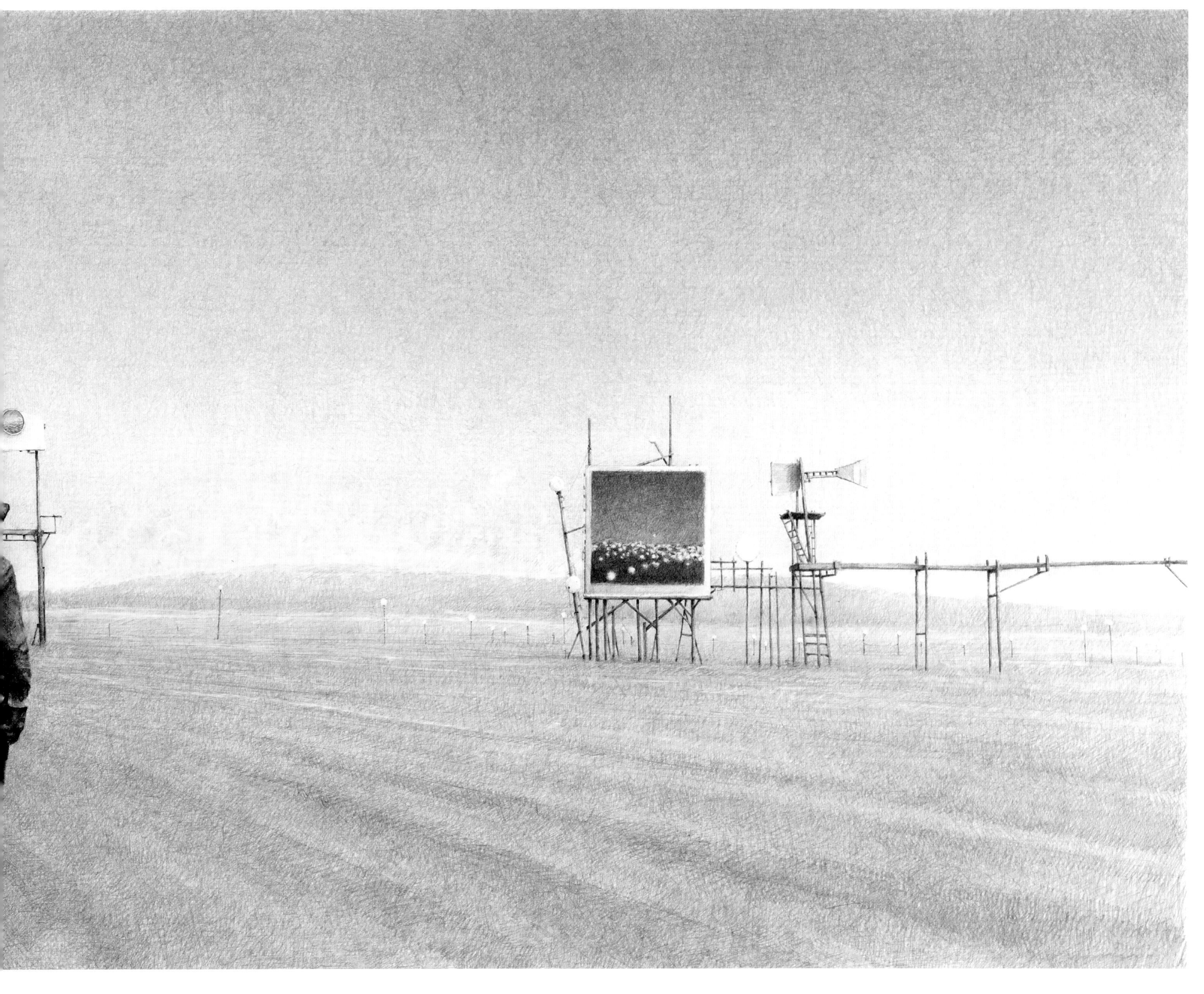

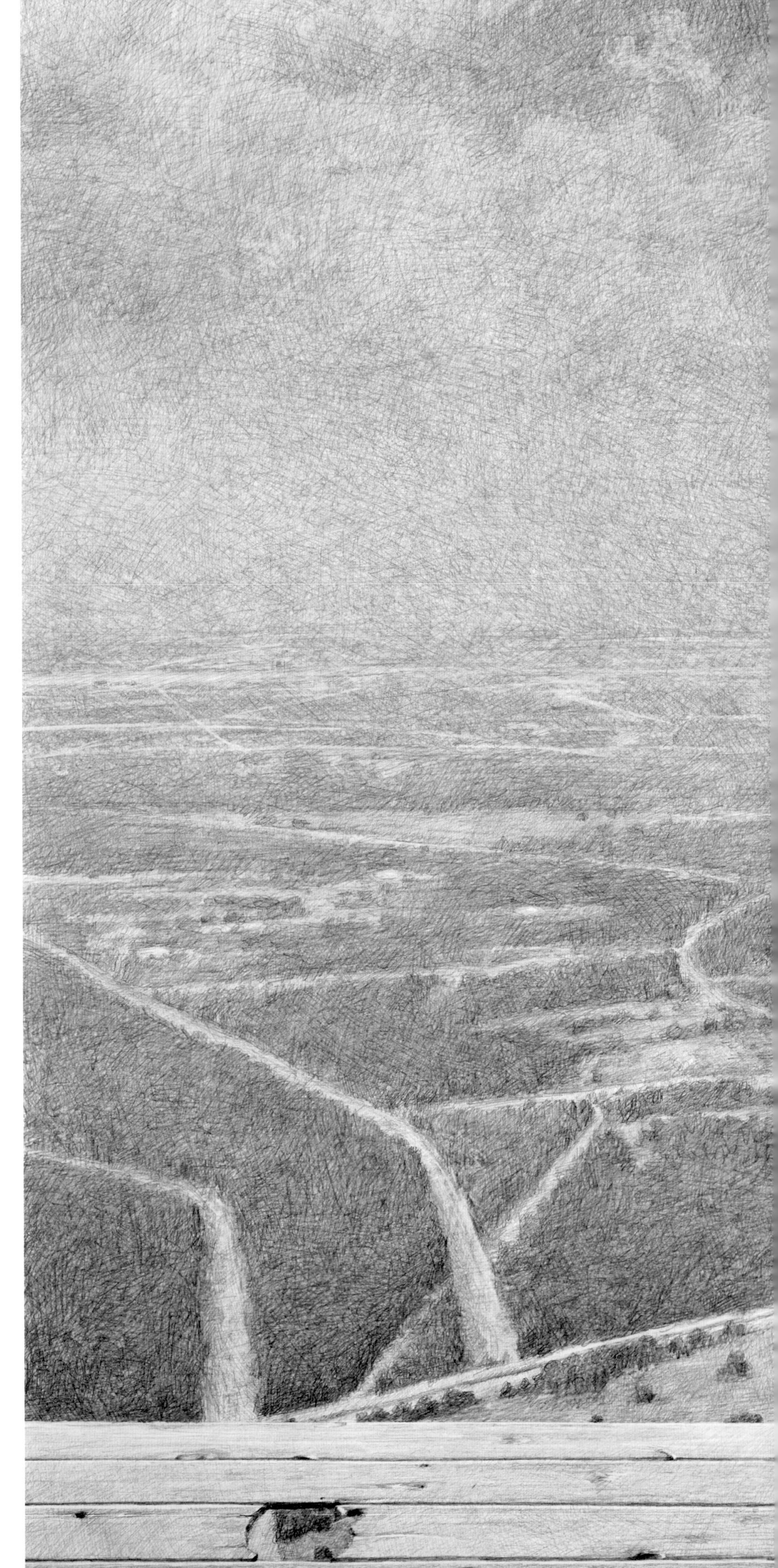

*Polyphonic*, detail

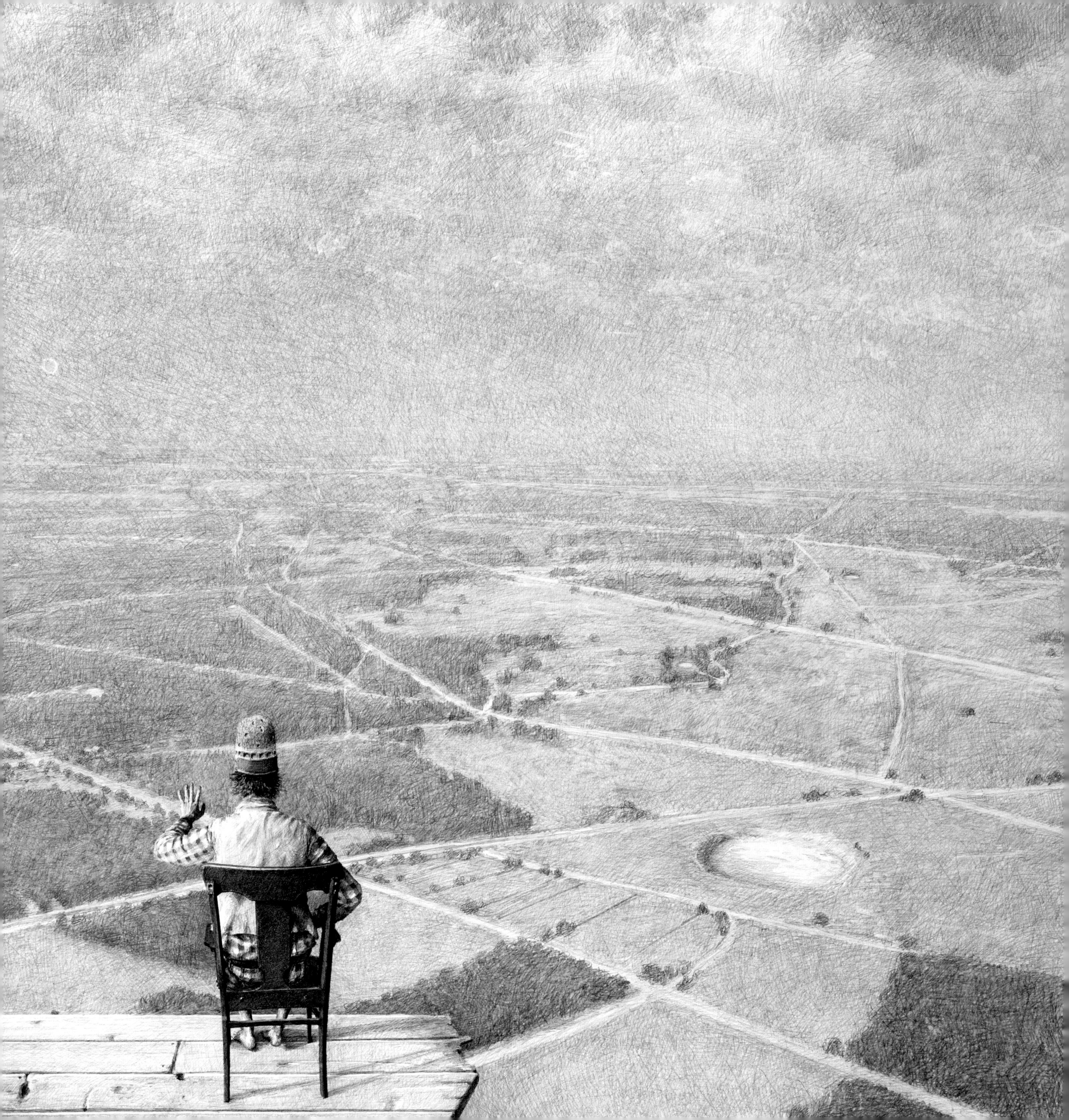

*It Moved Again*

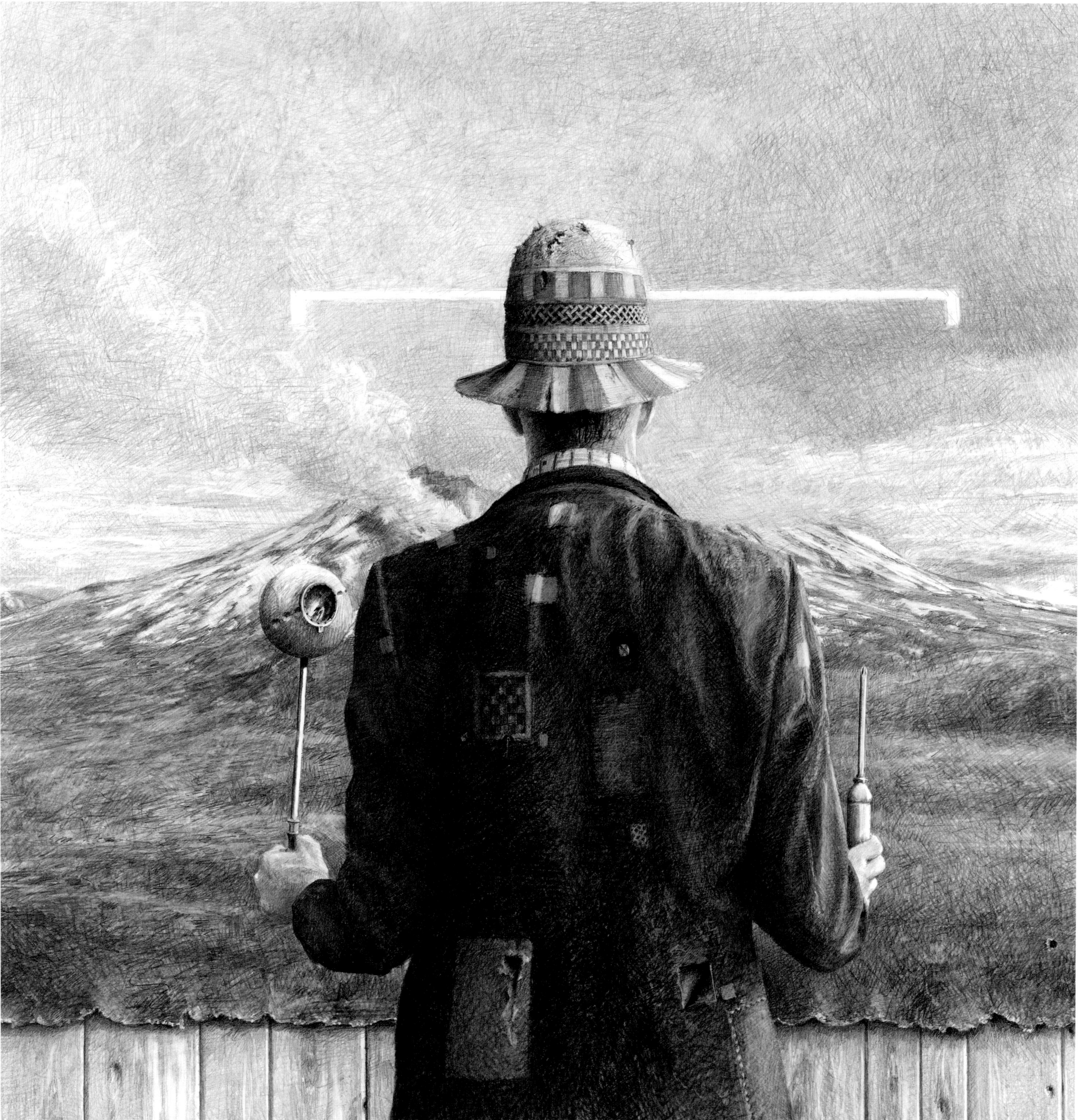

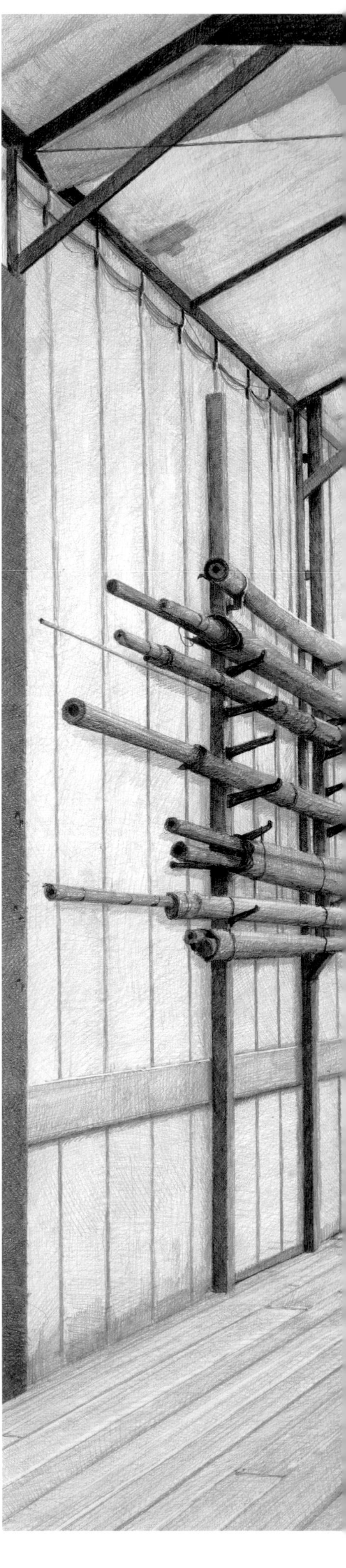

General Curtis Méliès

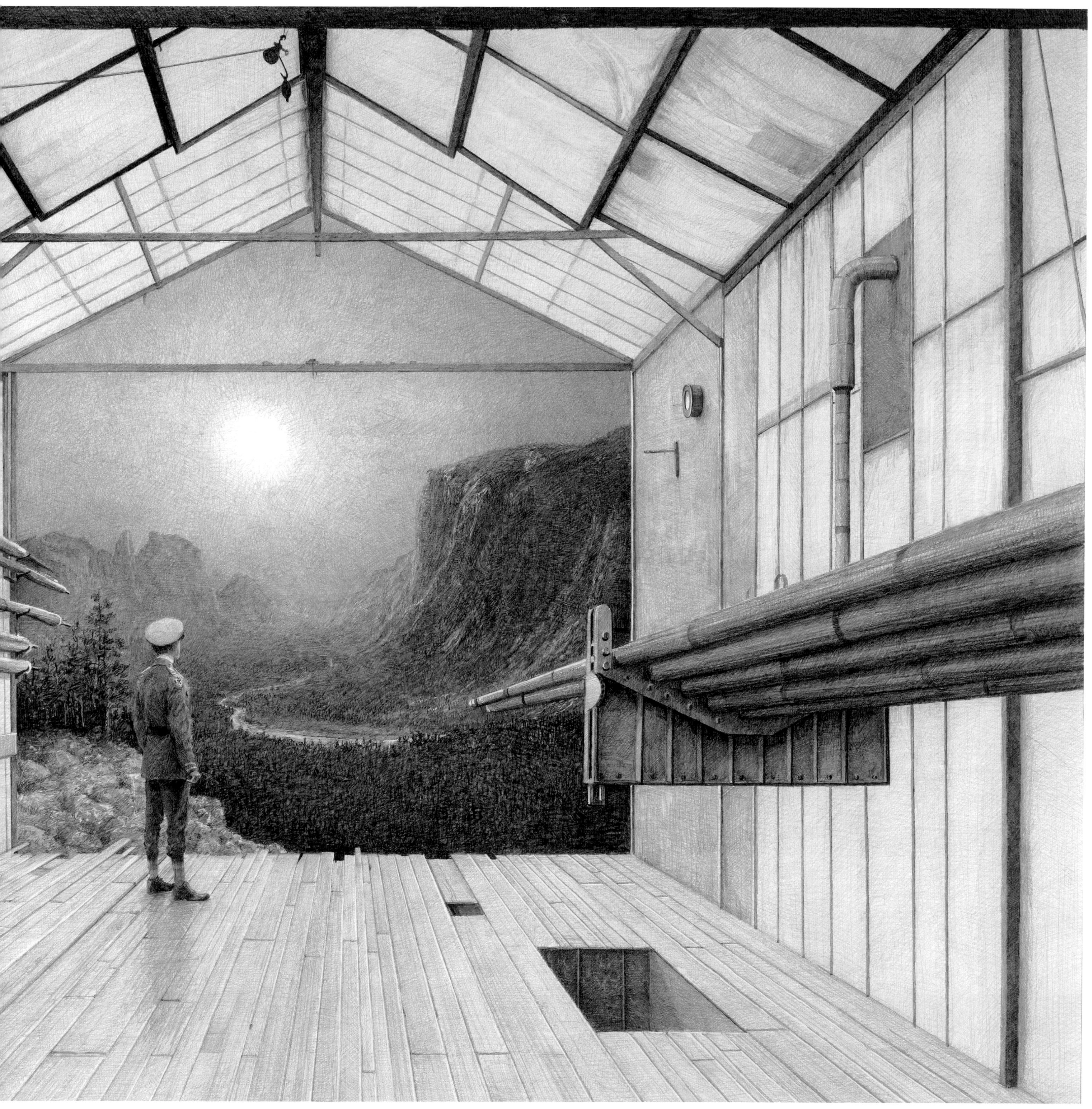

*Columbia River Beehive*

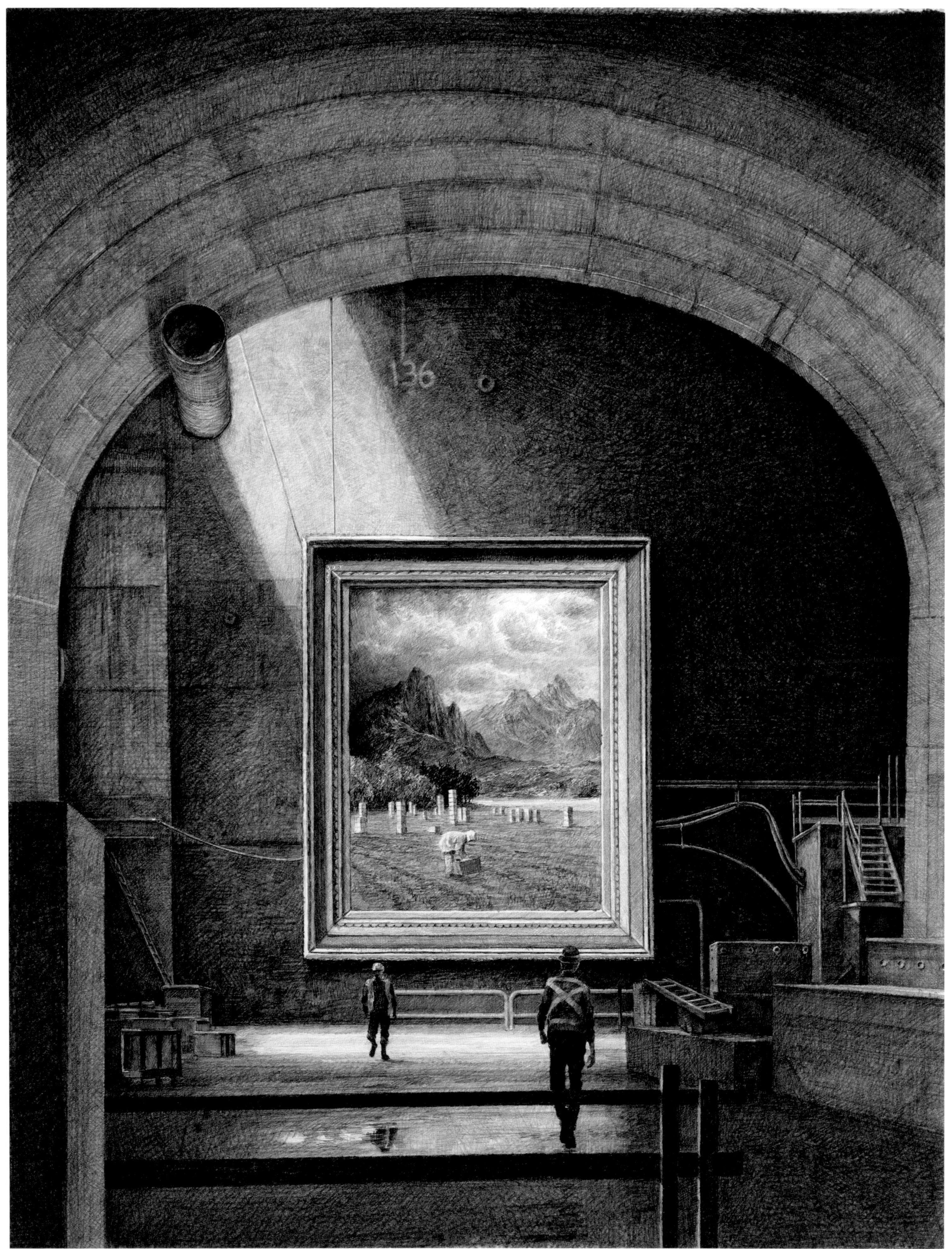
136

*And They Stirred*

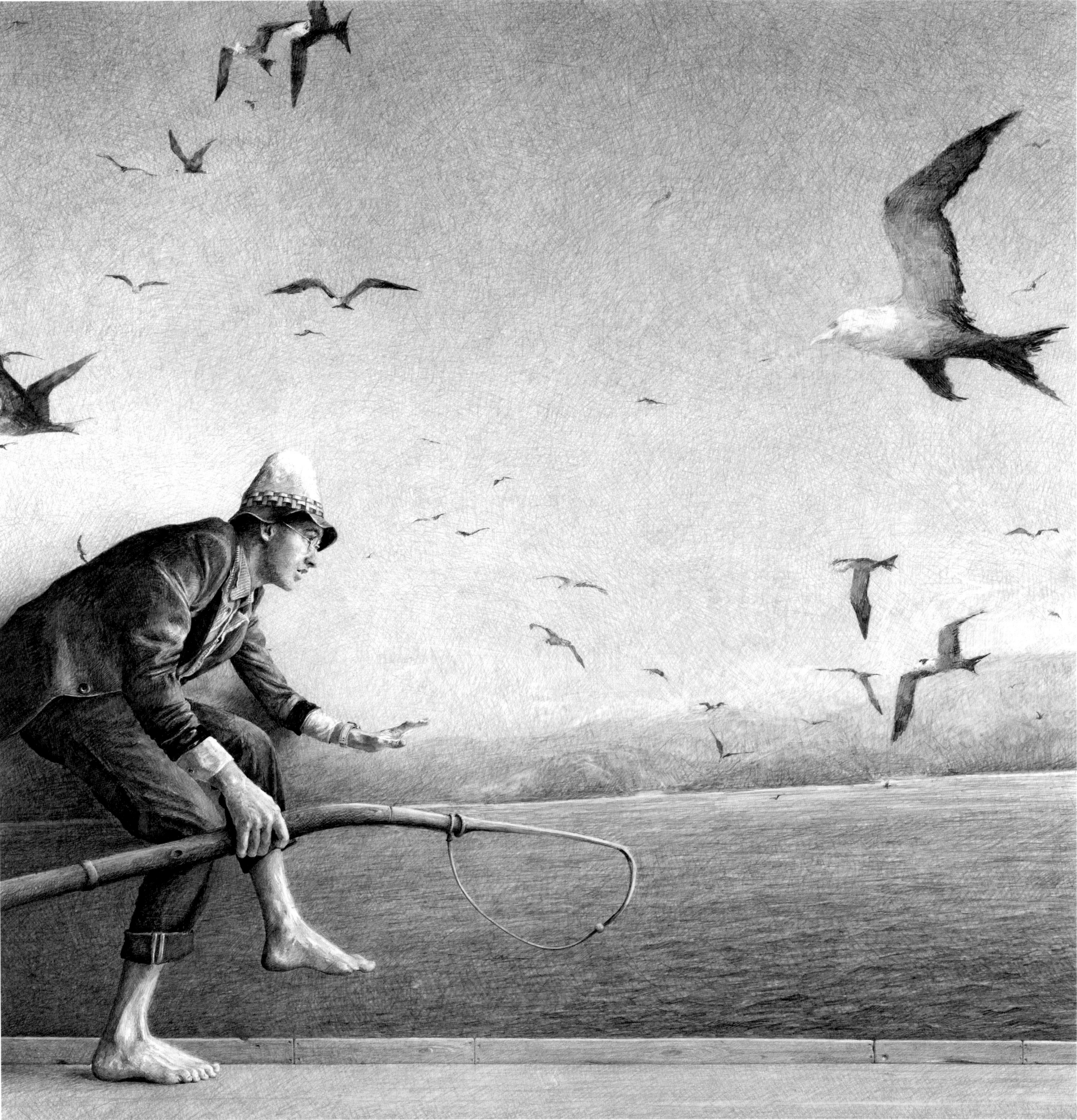

# Interior Monologue

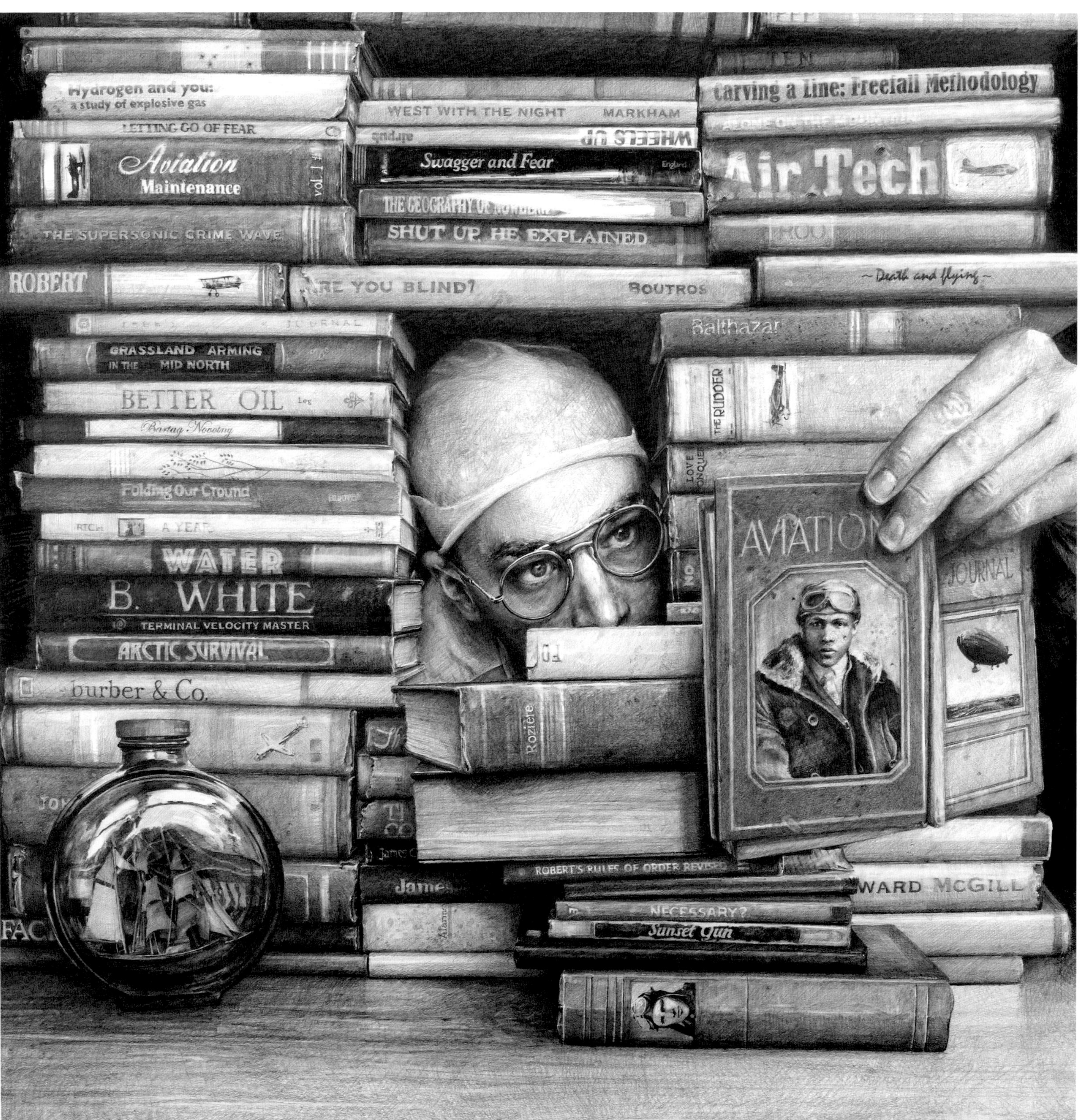
Hydrogen and you:
a study of explosive gas
LETTING GO OF FEAR
Aviation
Maintenance
THE SUPERSONIC CRIME WAVE
ROBERT
ARE YOU BLIND?
BOUTROS
WEST WITH THE NIGHT
MARKHAM
WHEELS UP
Swagger and Fear
THE GEOGRAPHY OF
SHUT UP, HE EXPLAINED
Carving a Line: Freefall Methodology
Air Tech
~ Death and flying ~
Balthazar
GRASSLAND ARMING
IN THE MID NORTH
BETTER OIL
Bartag Novotny
Folding Our Ground
A YEAR
WATER
B. WHITE
TERMINAL VELOCITY MASTER
ARCTIC SURVIVAL
burber & Co.
THE RUDDER
AVIATION
JOURNAL
Rozière
ROBERT'S RULES OF ORDER REVISE
NECESSARY?
Sunset Gun
WARD McGILL
James

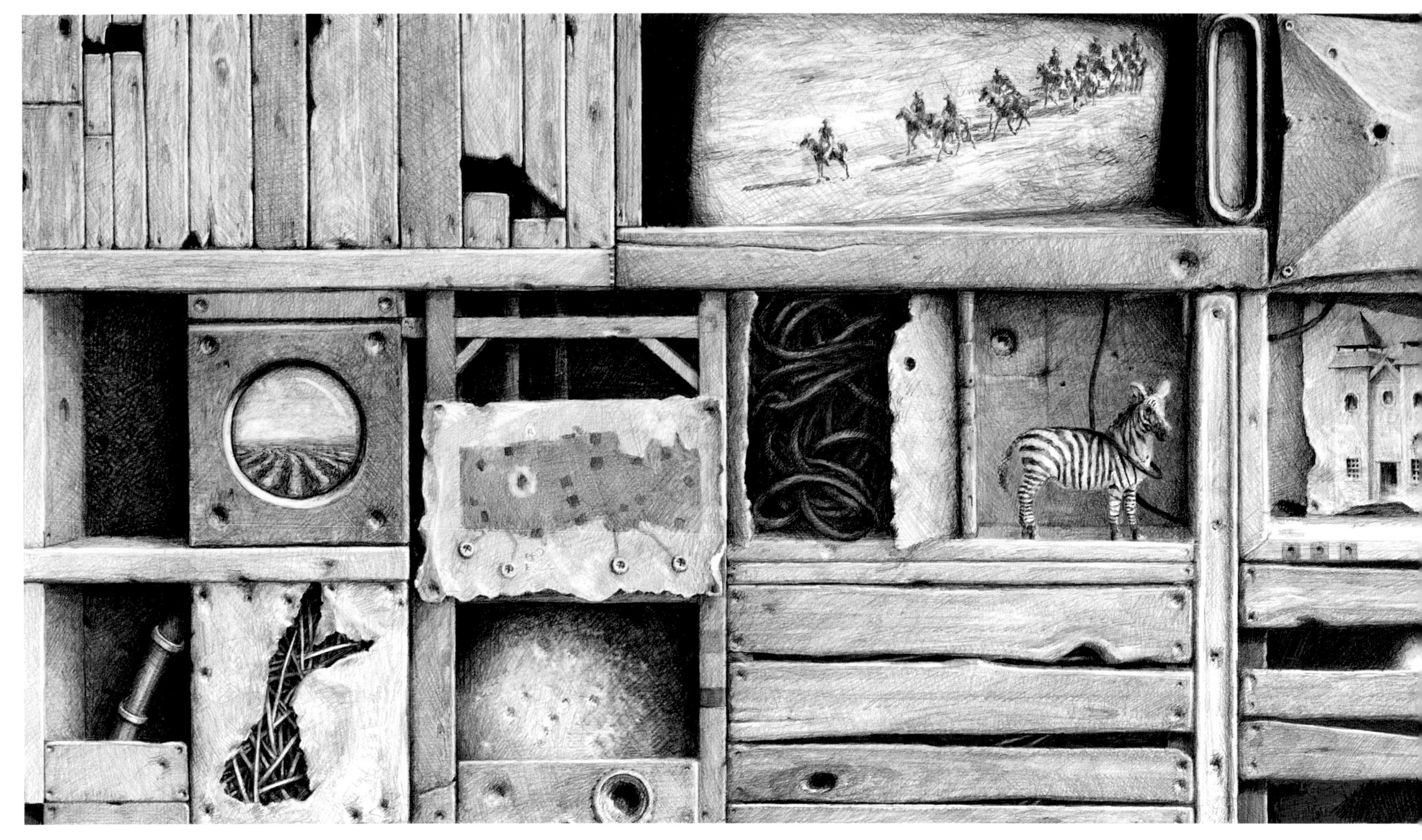

Previous page:
*Speed Reading Quota Enlarged during Inclement Weather*

*The Prisoners*

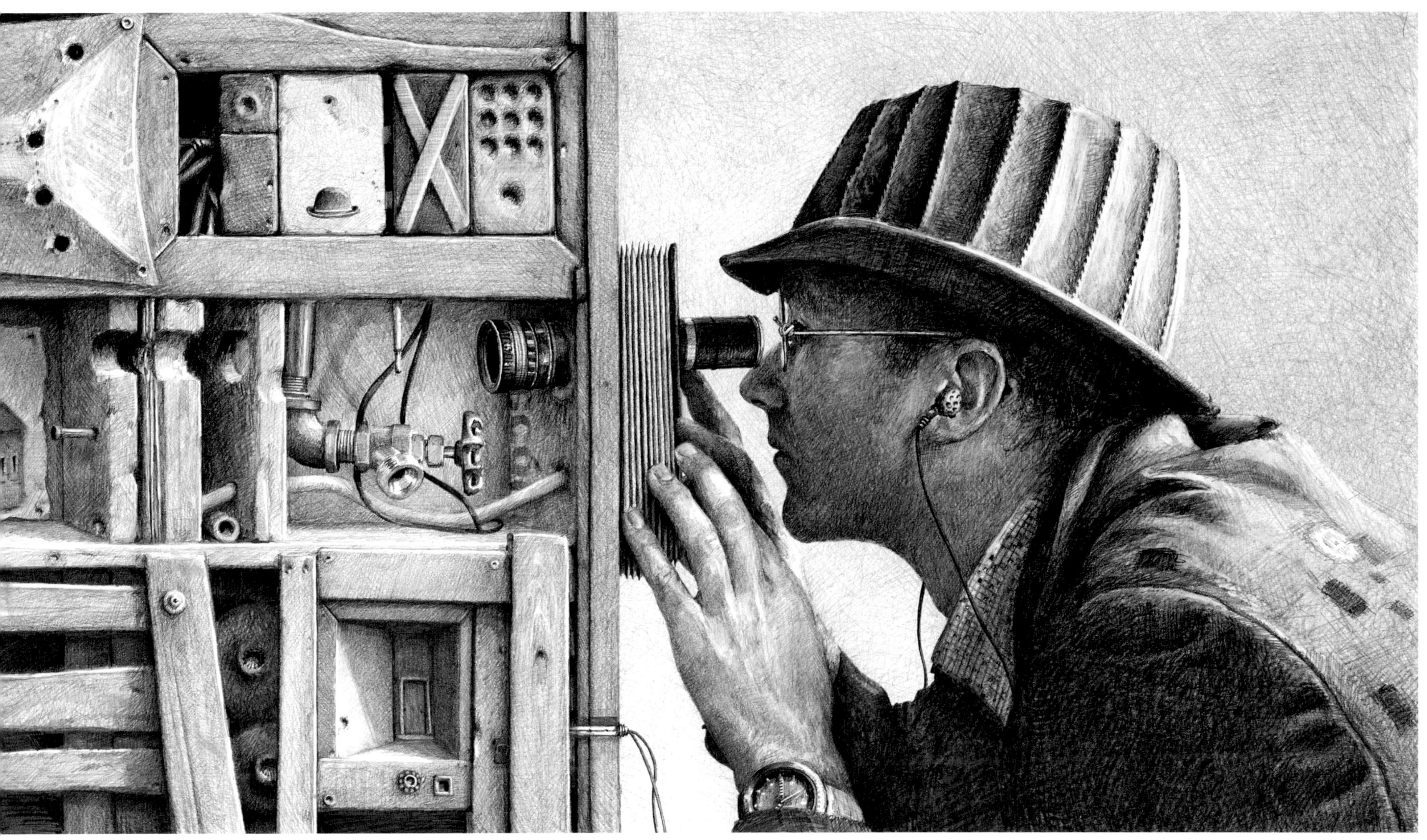

Raw Diet Increasing Audacity and Night Vision

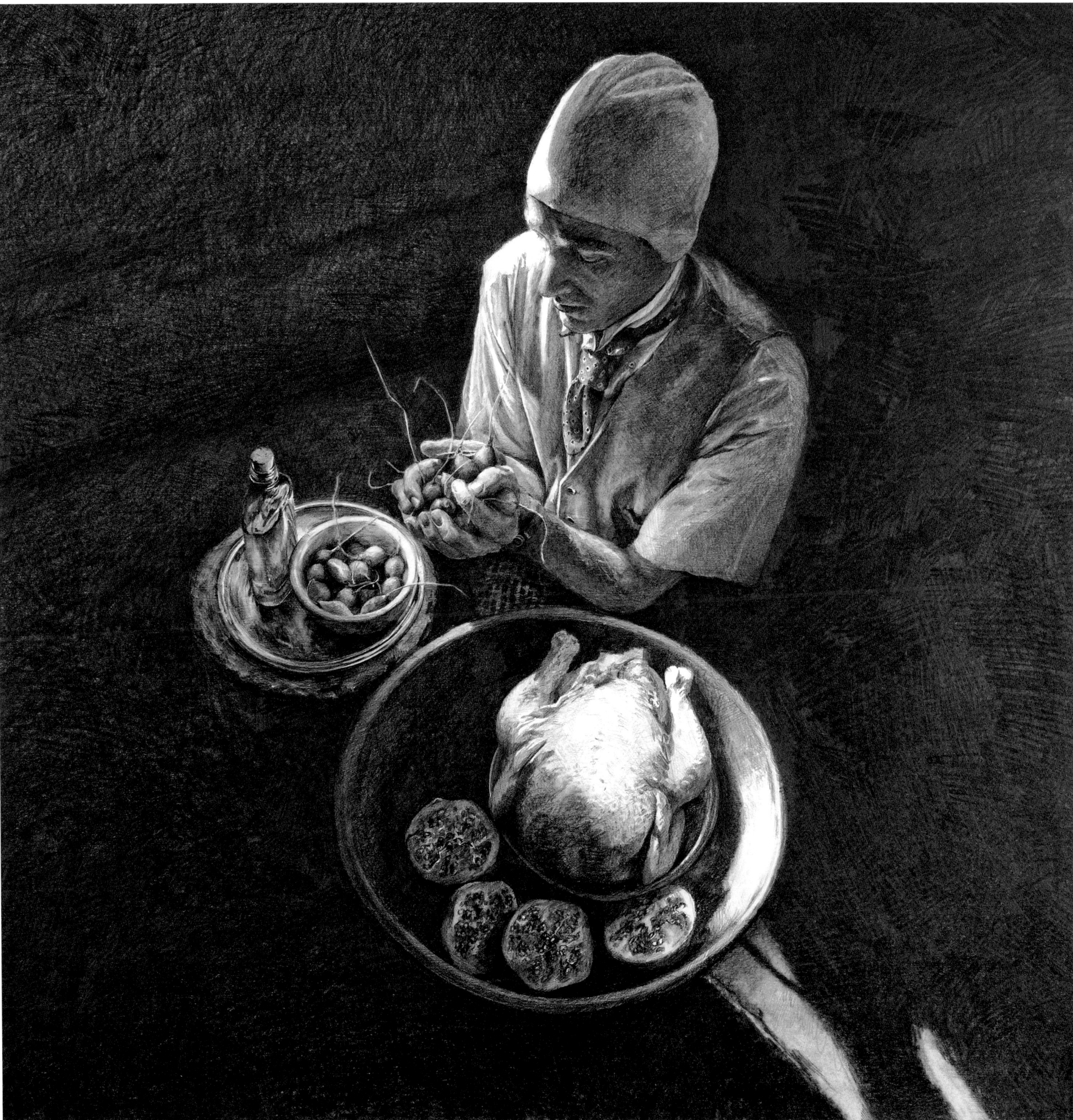

Obelix

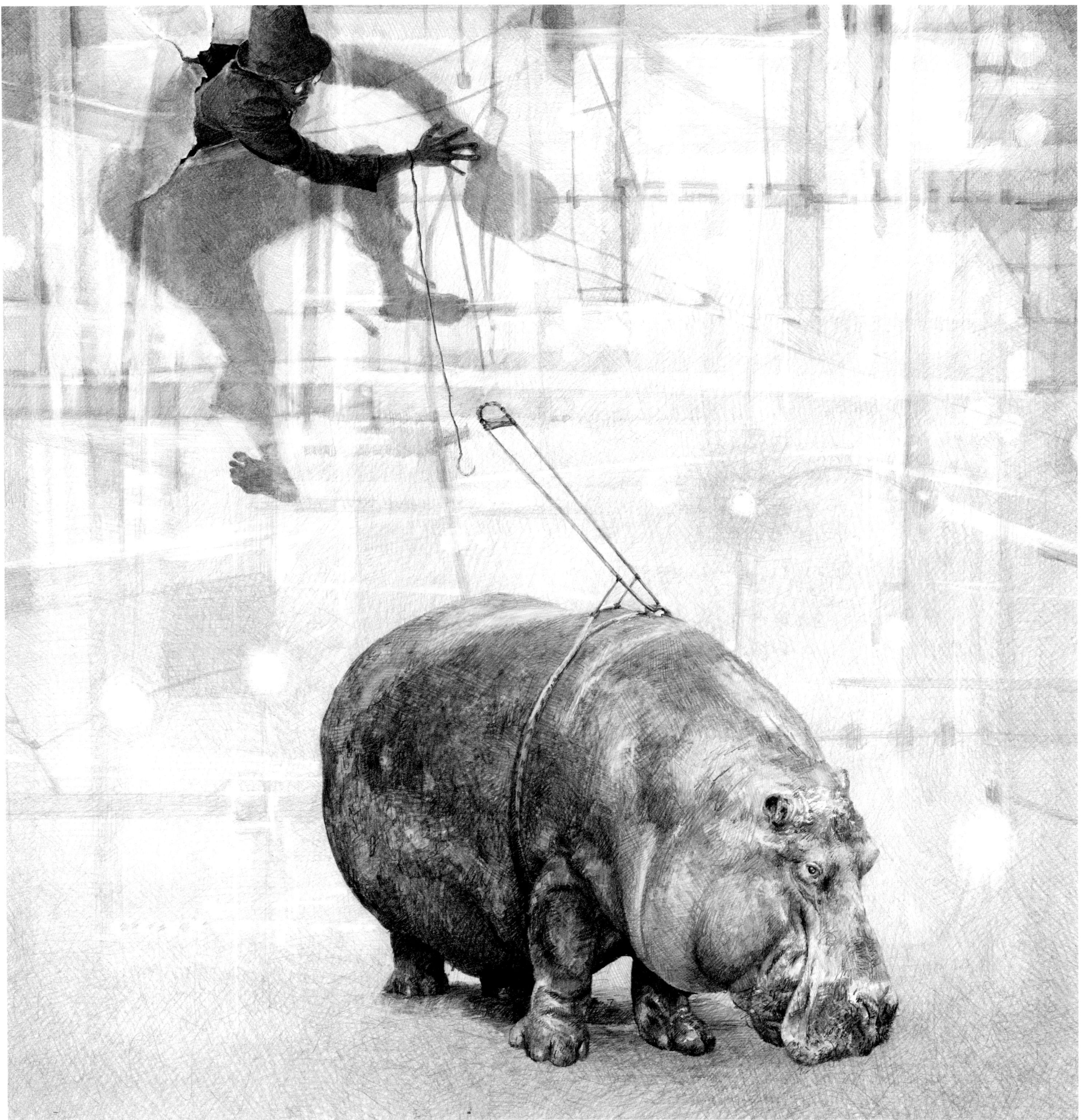

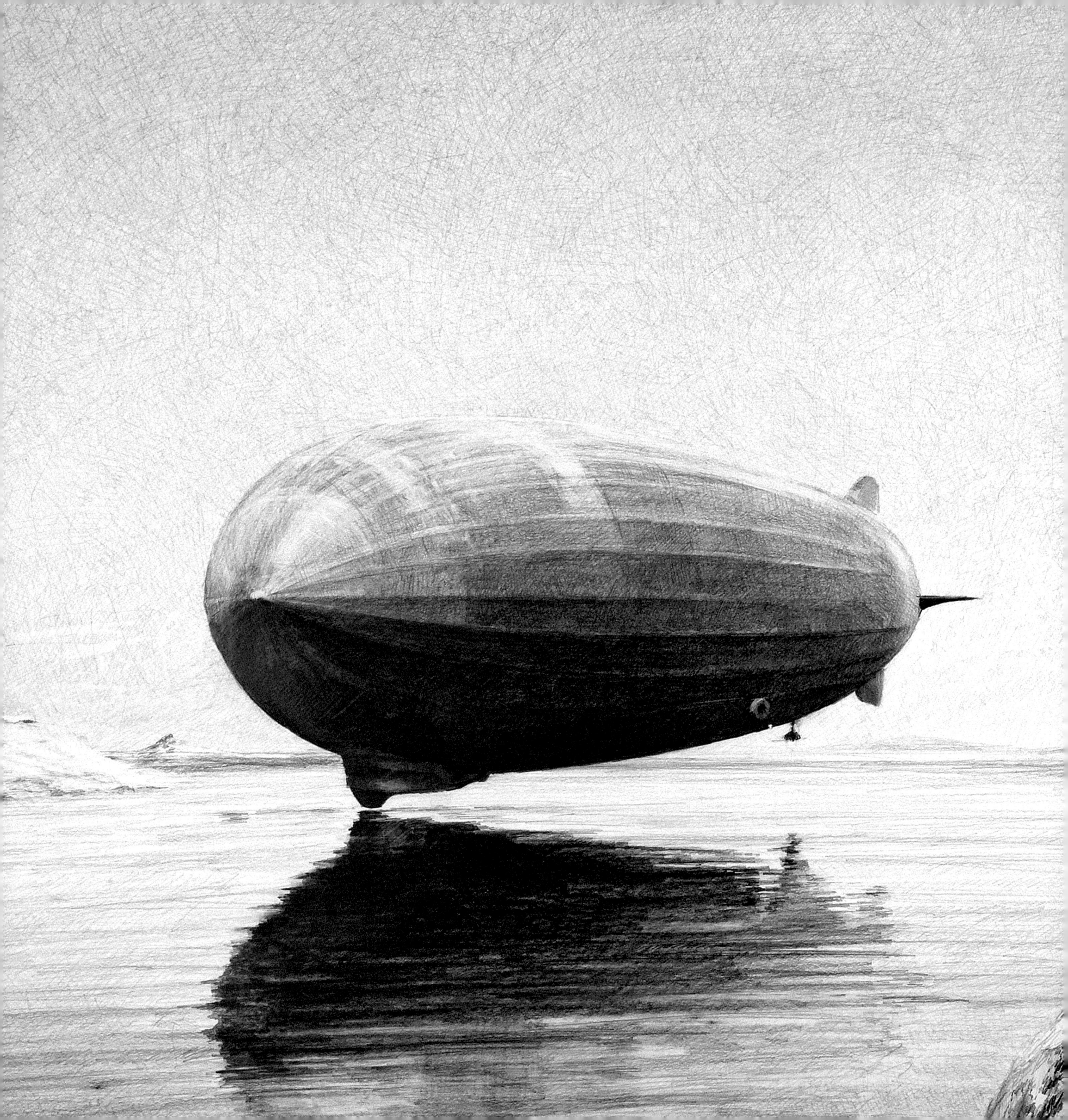

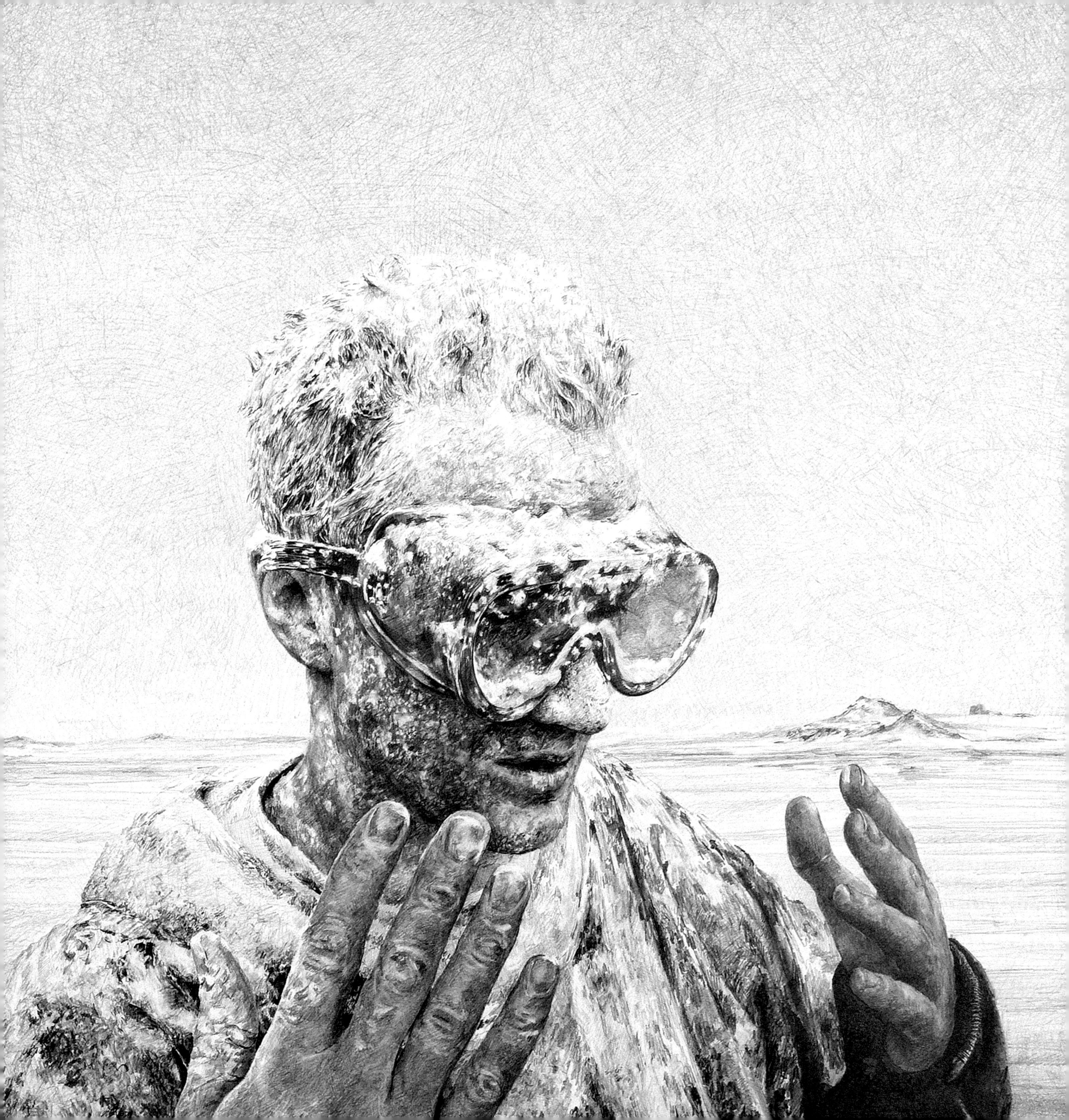

Previous pages:
*Negligible Frostnip during Baffin Bay Freefall*, detail

*An Iron Roller Coaster Rose Out of the Tundra and Quite a Few Wondered Why but No One Said a Word*

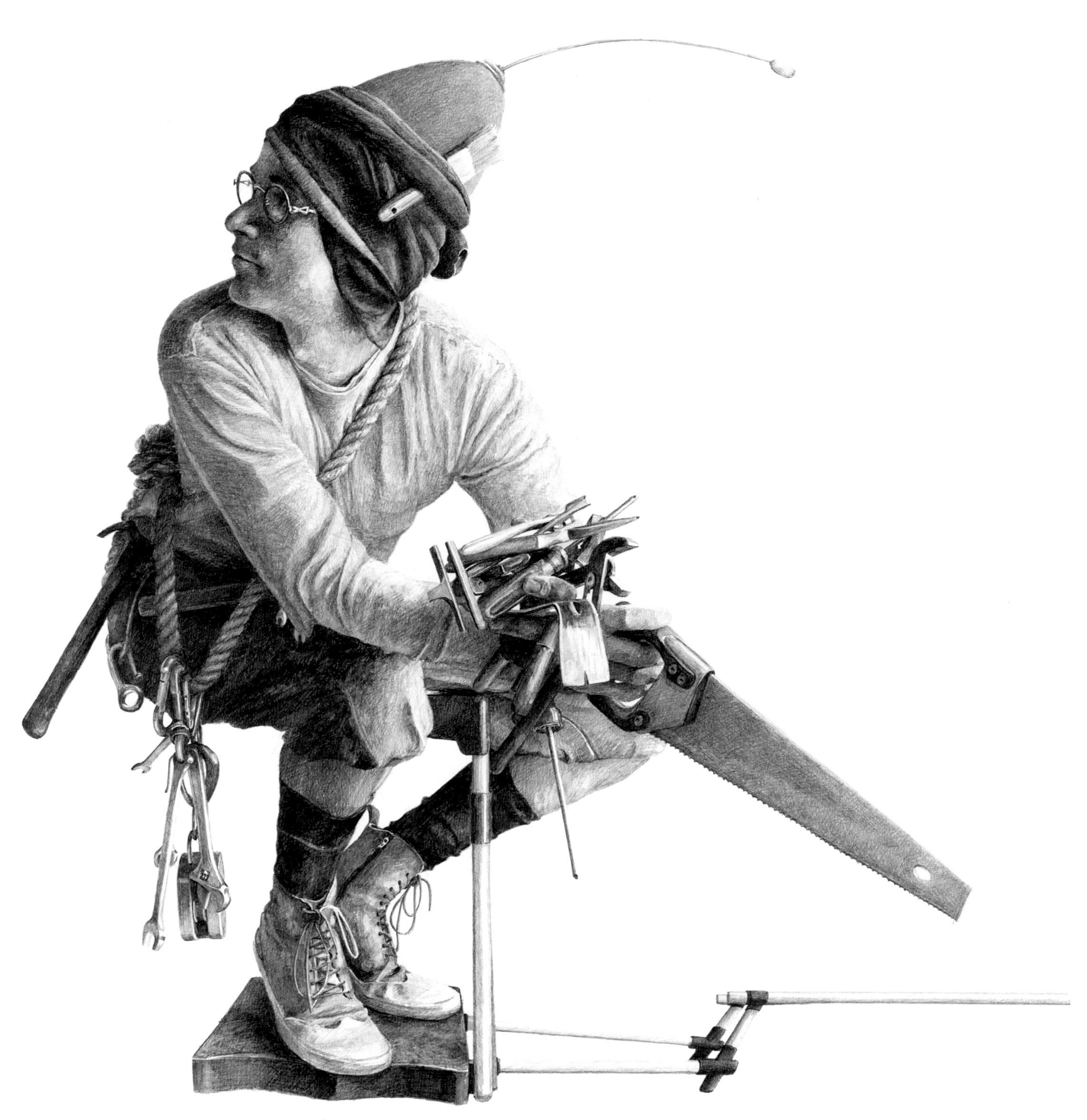

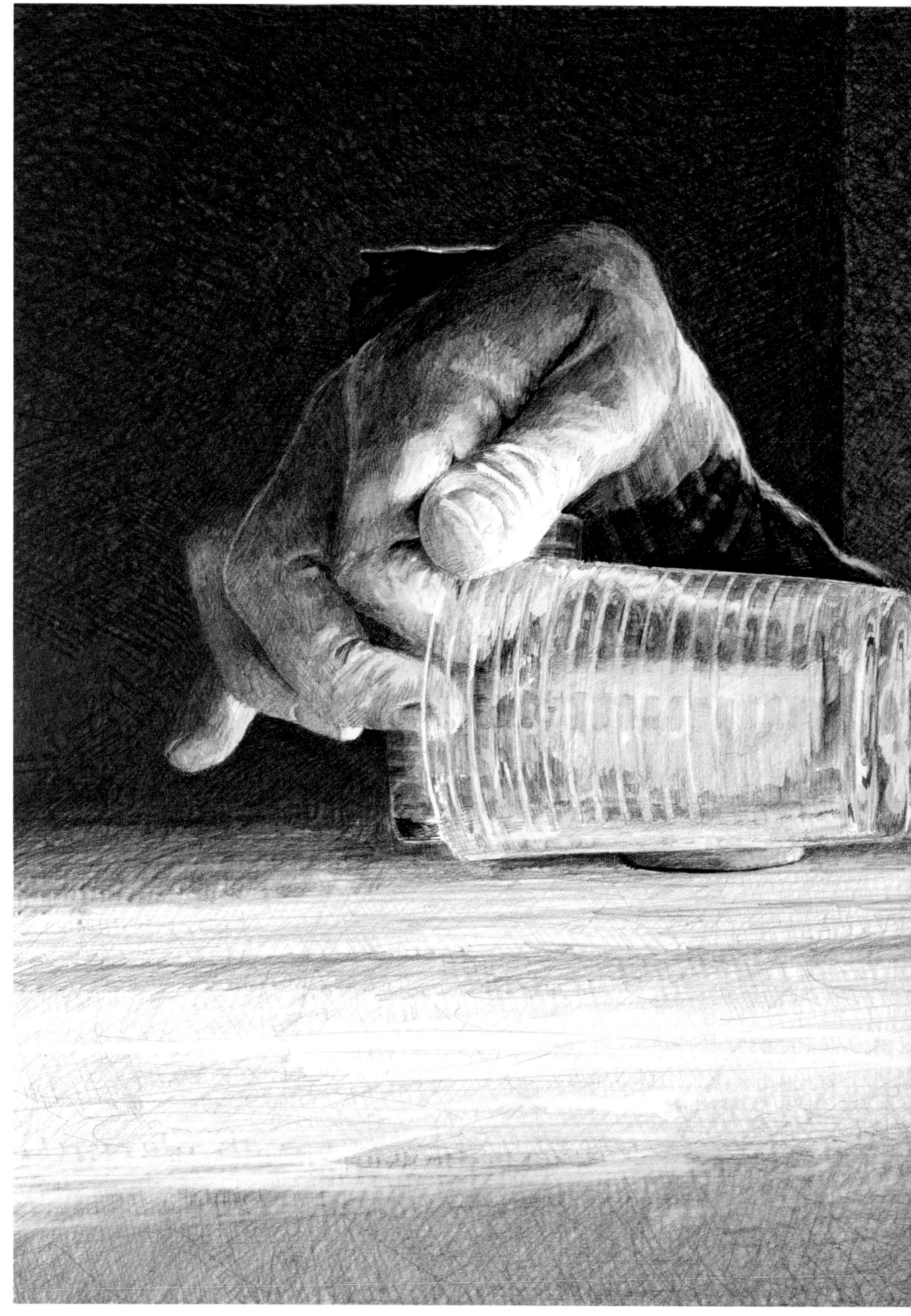

*Error*

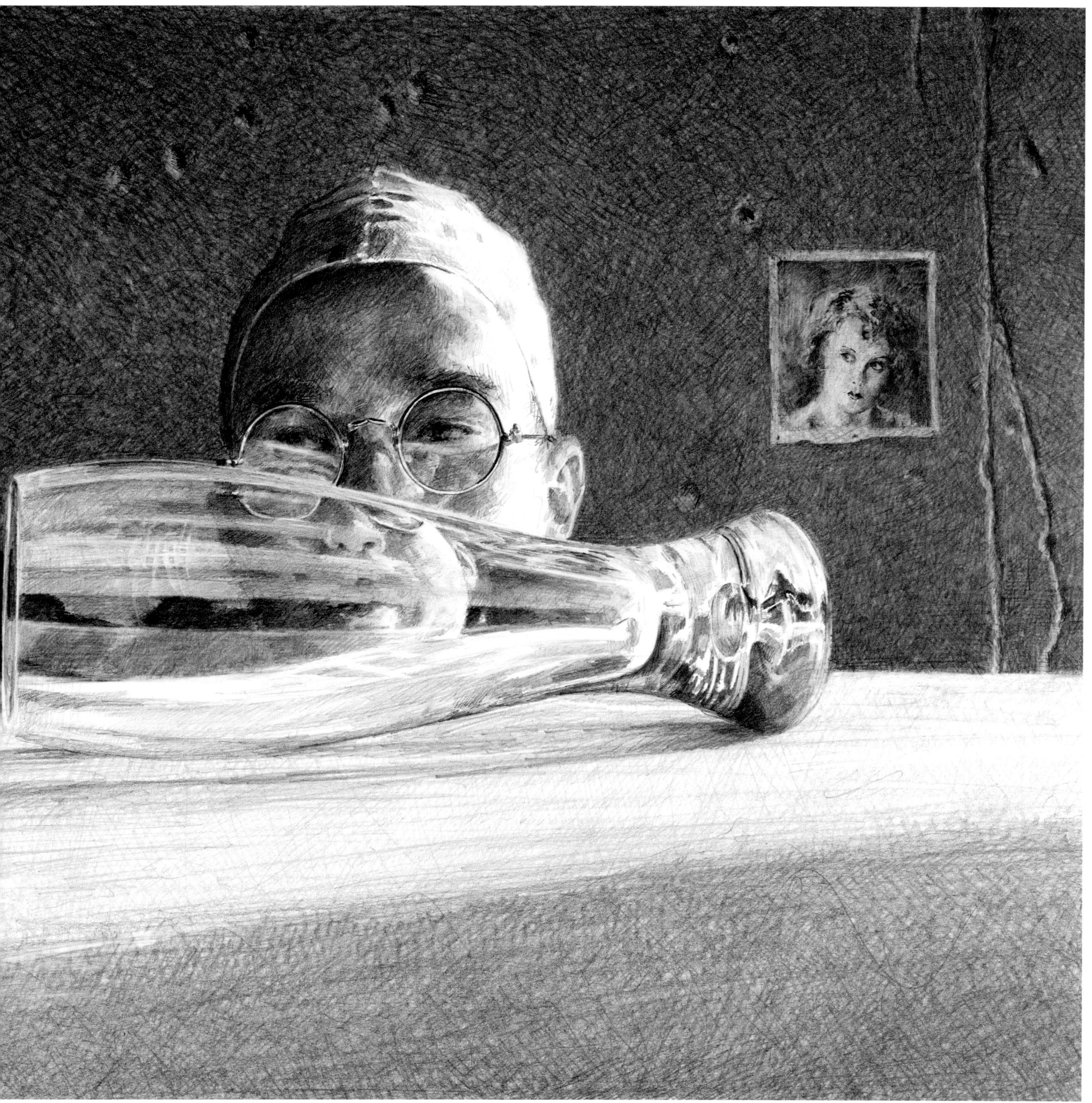

*Crimean War*

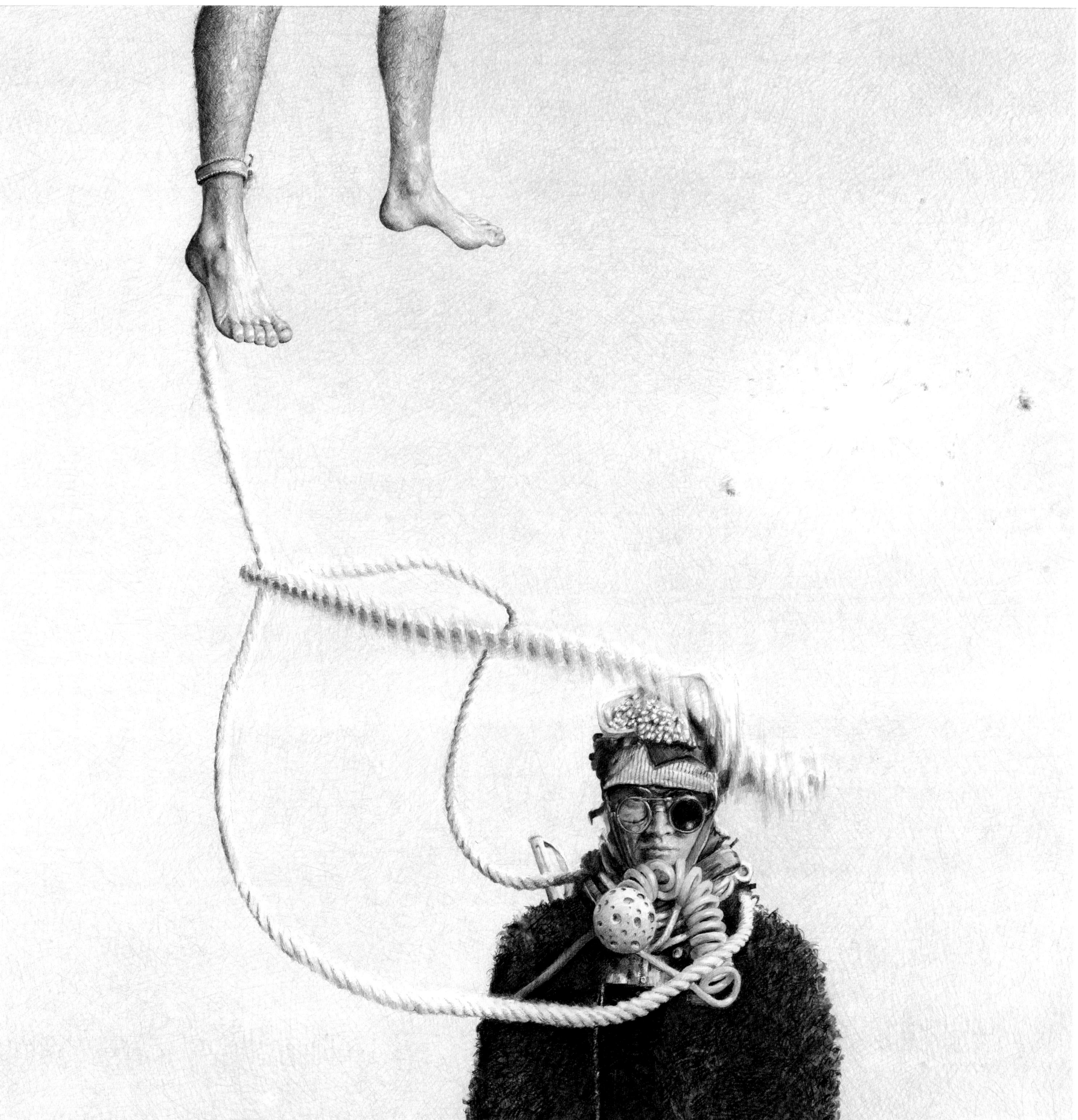

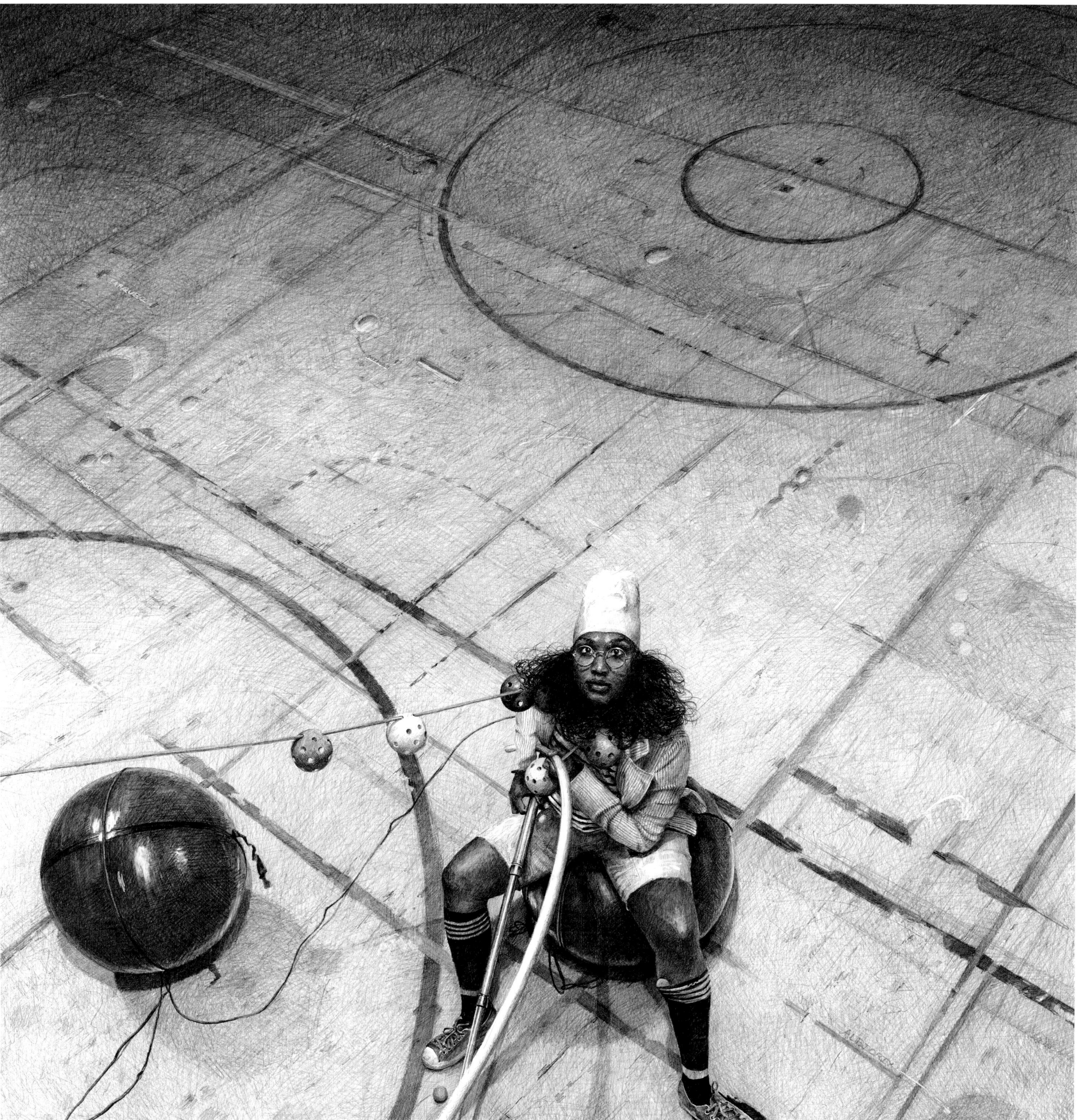

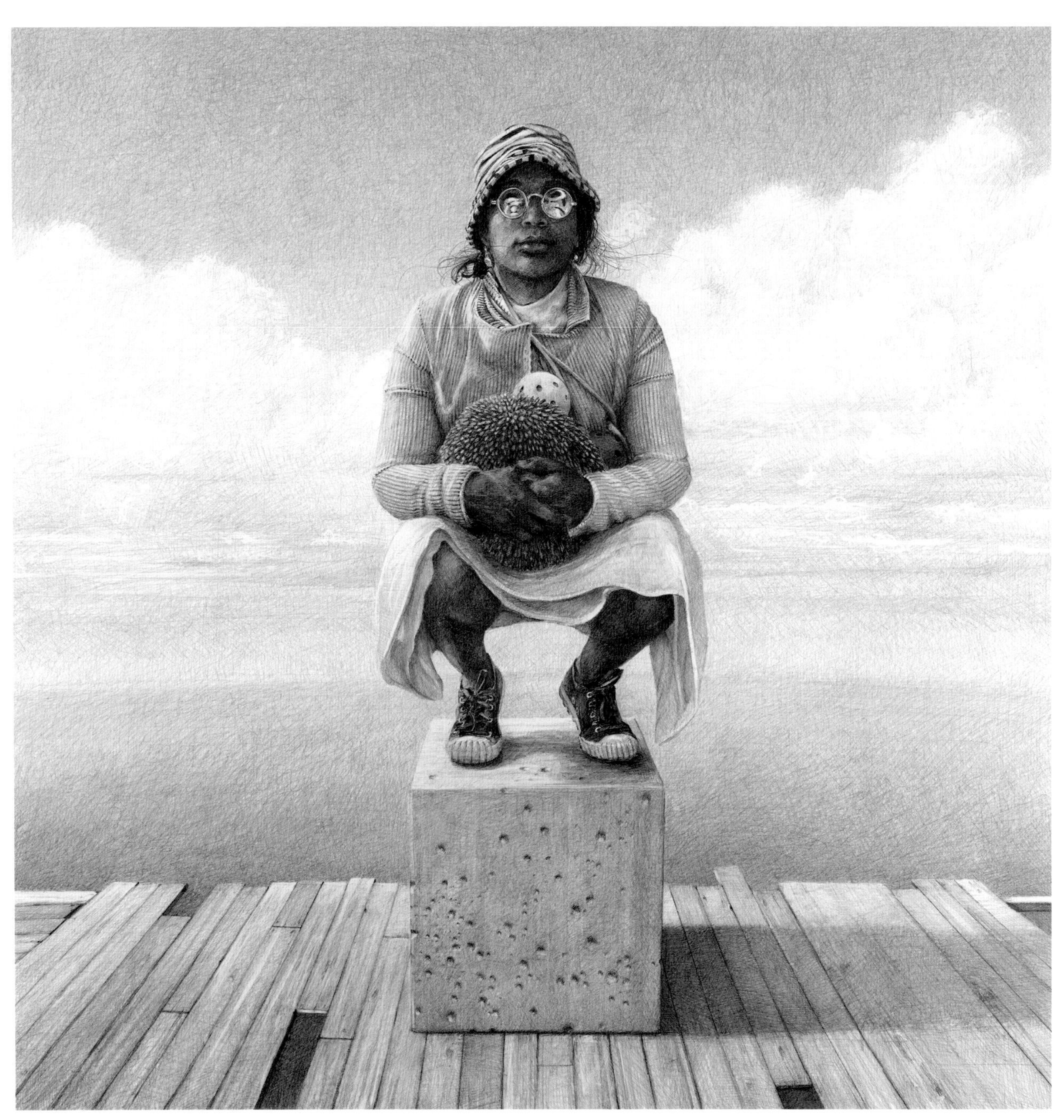

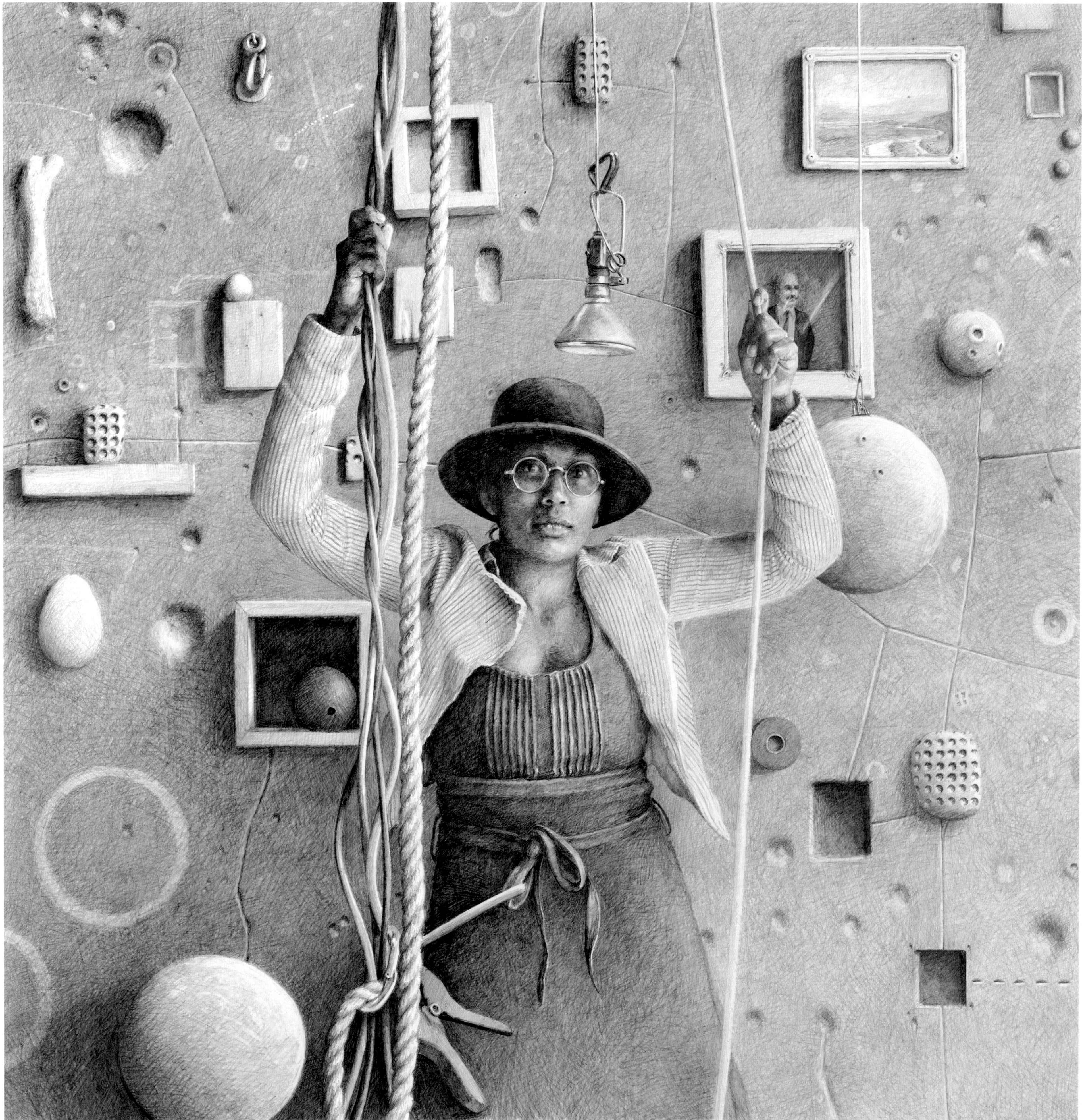

*Previous pages:*
*Will Be Snaring Meteorites – And Win the War Game of the Sky*
*Will Be Snaring Meteorites – And Build a Library of Success*

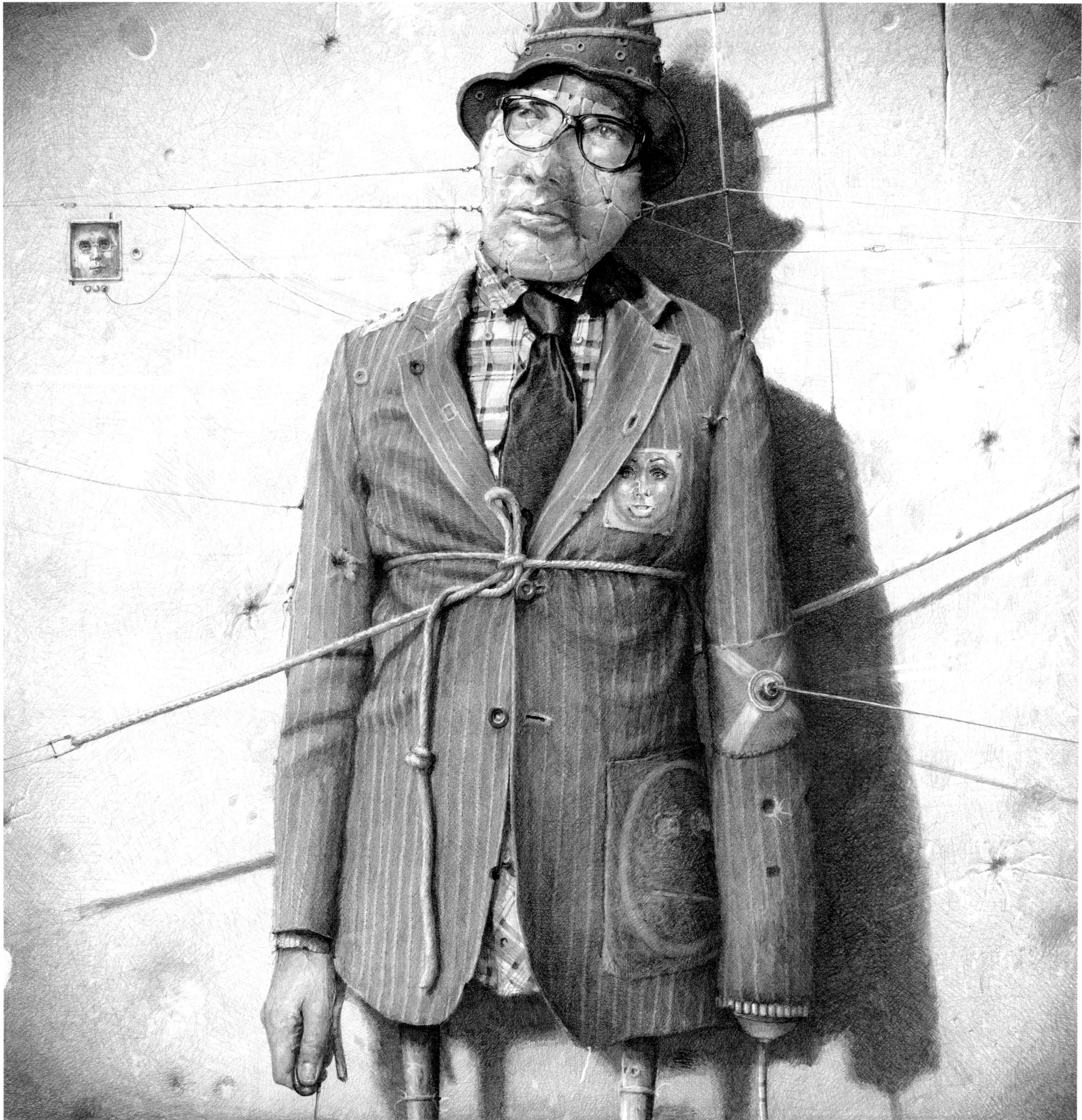

*Fresh and Strong the World We Seize*, detail

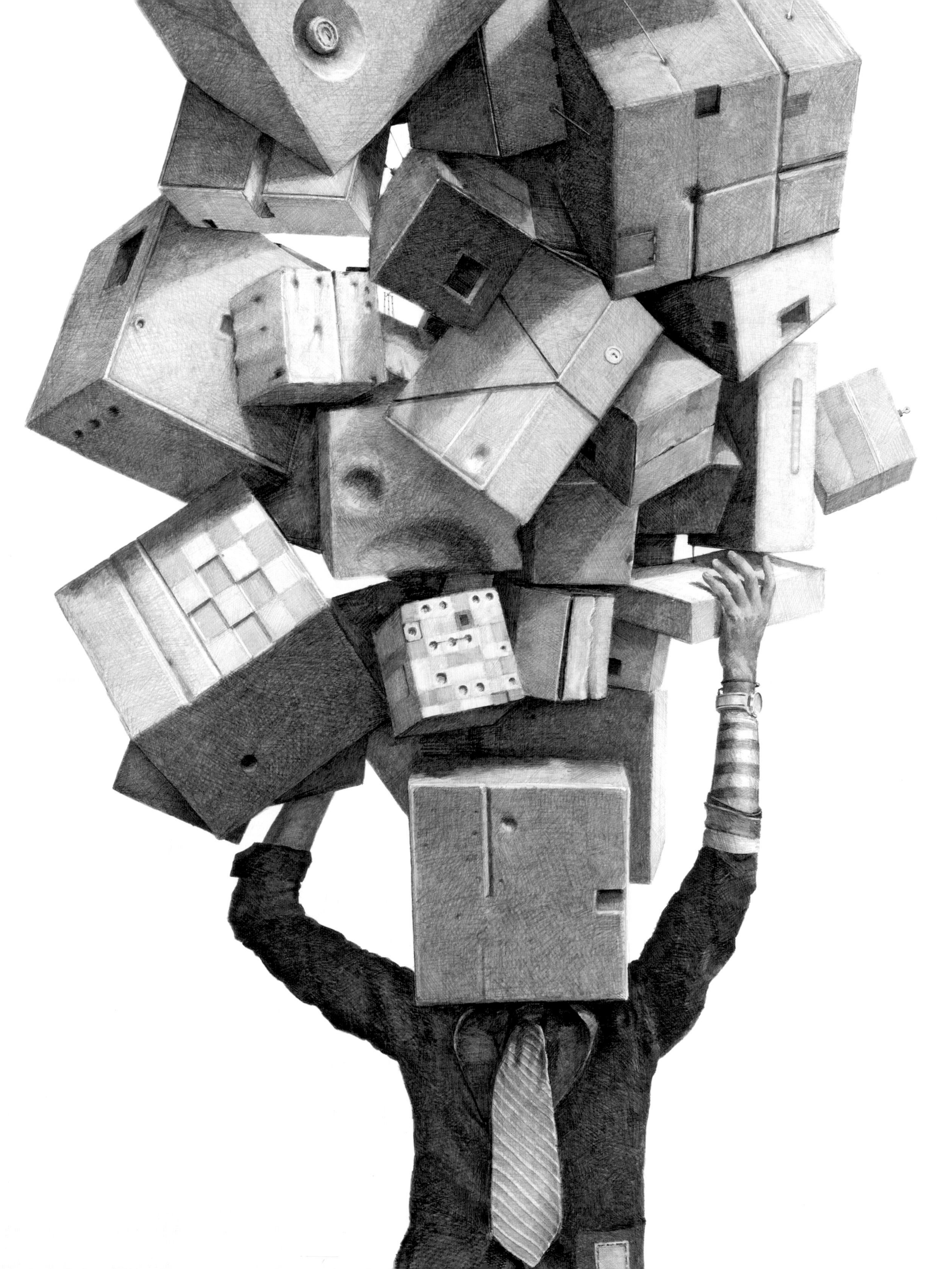

Narcissus

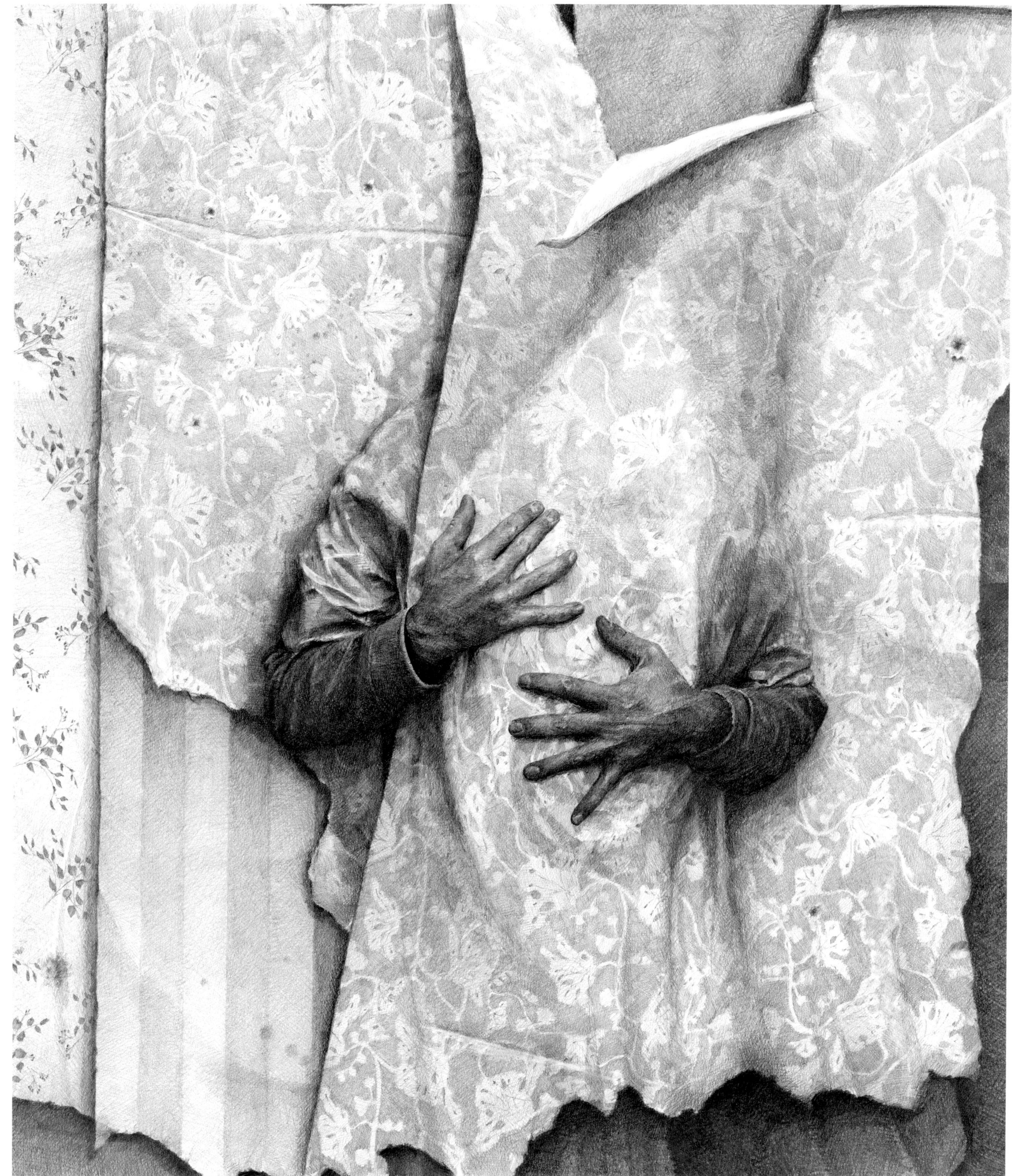

*Himself Mourning Himself Made for an Awkward Wake*

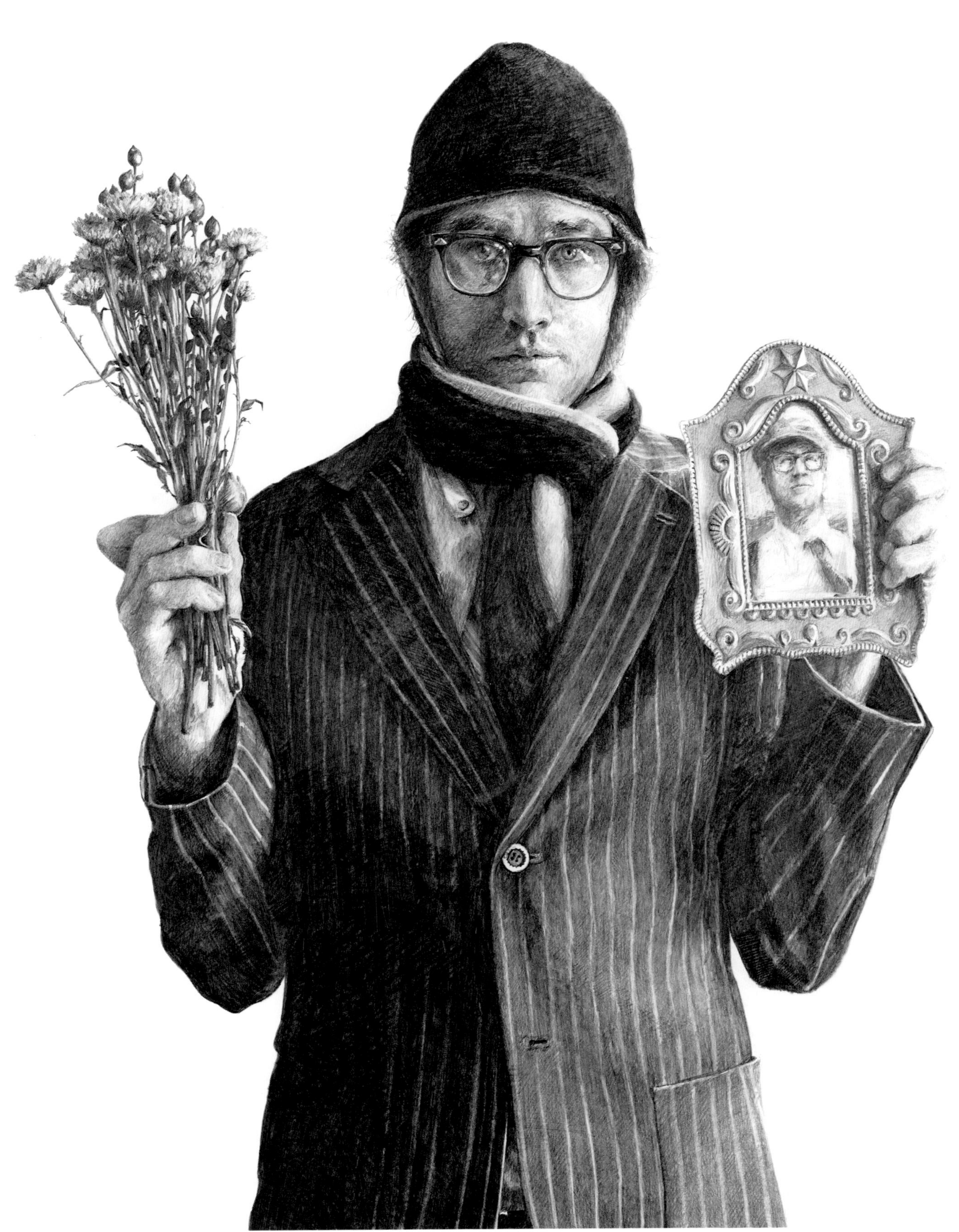

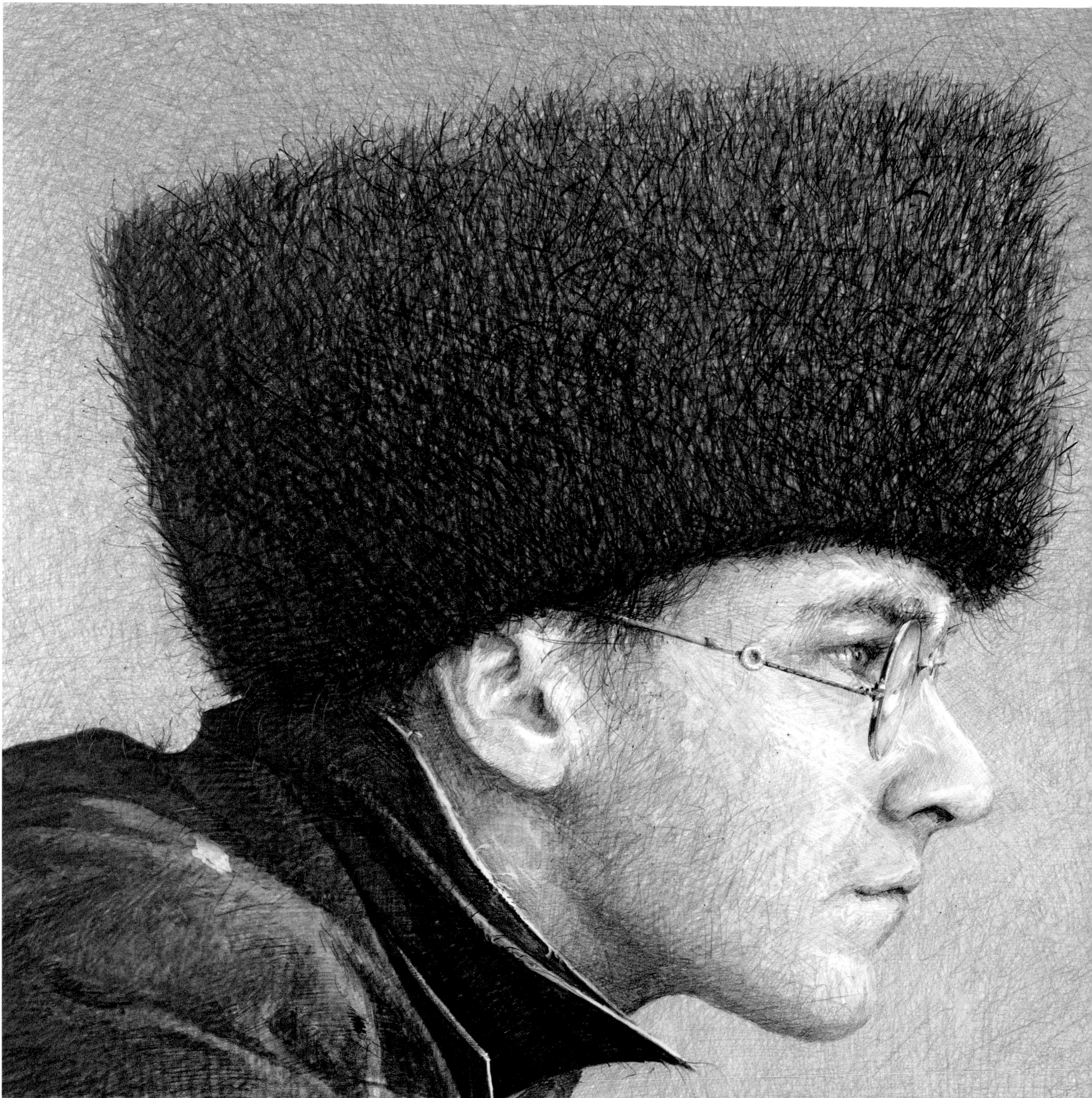

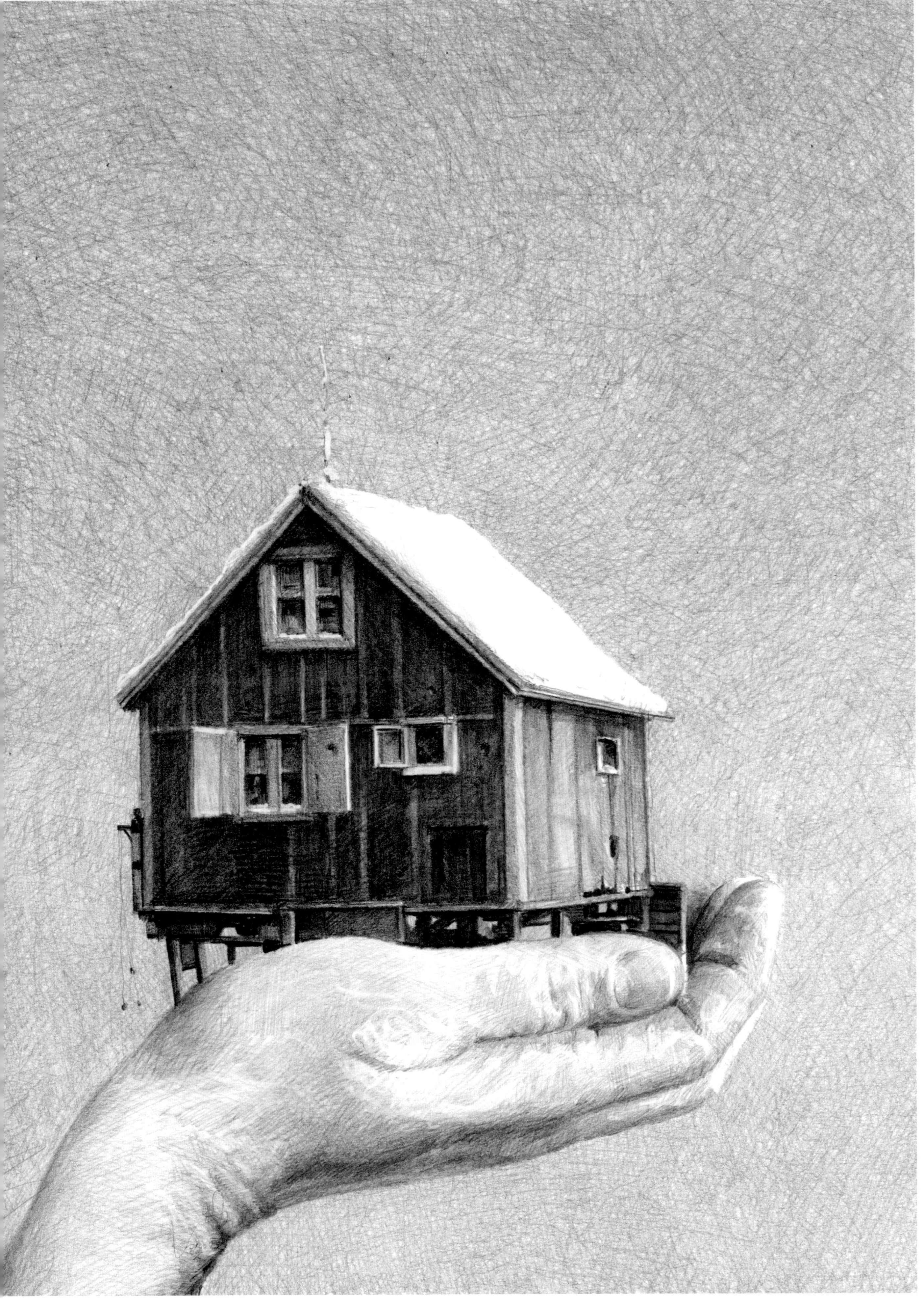

*The Furnace*

*To Atlantis*

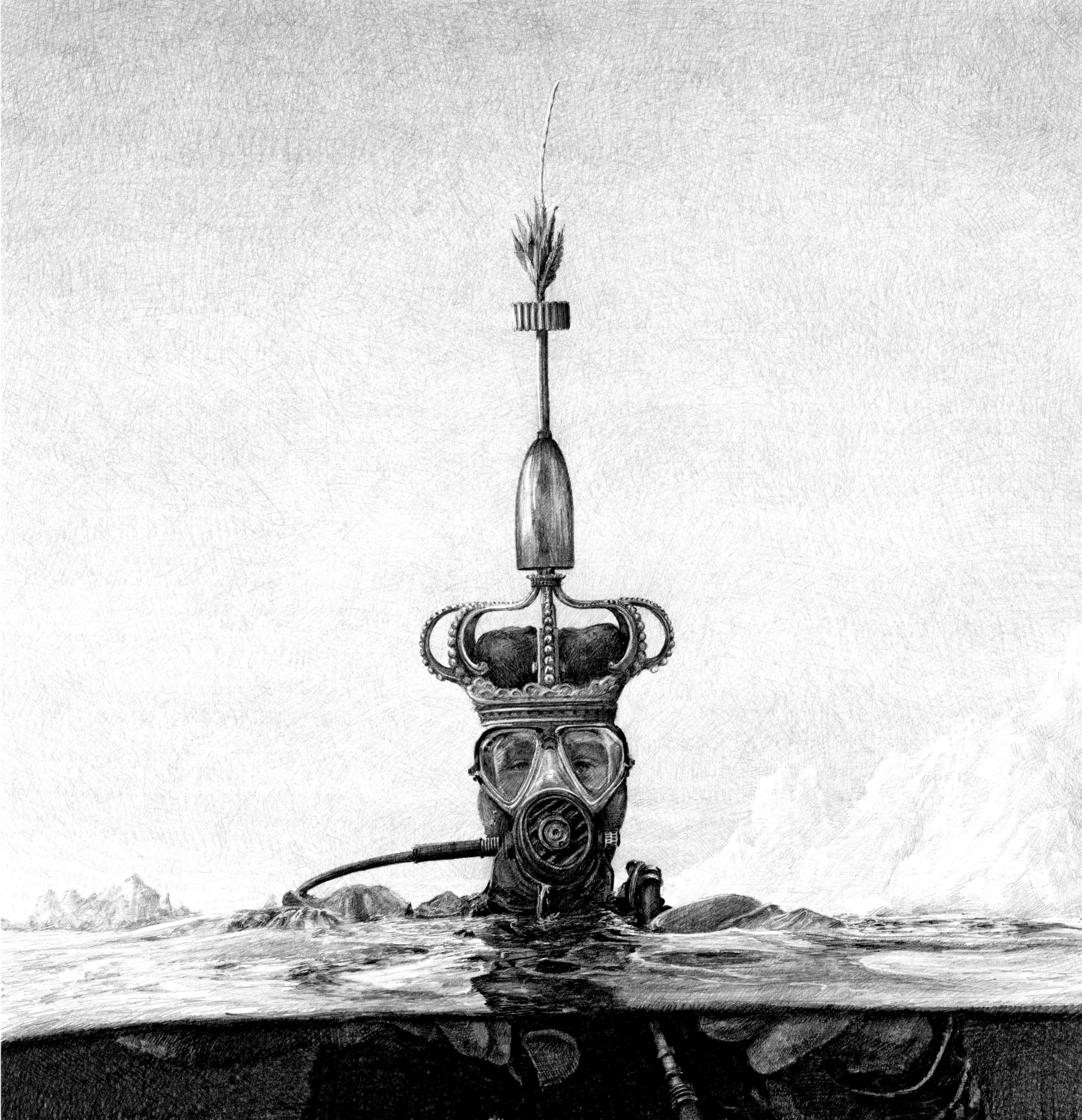

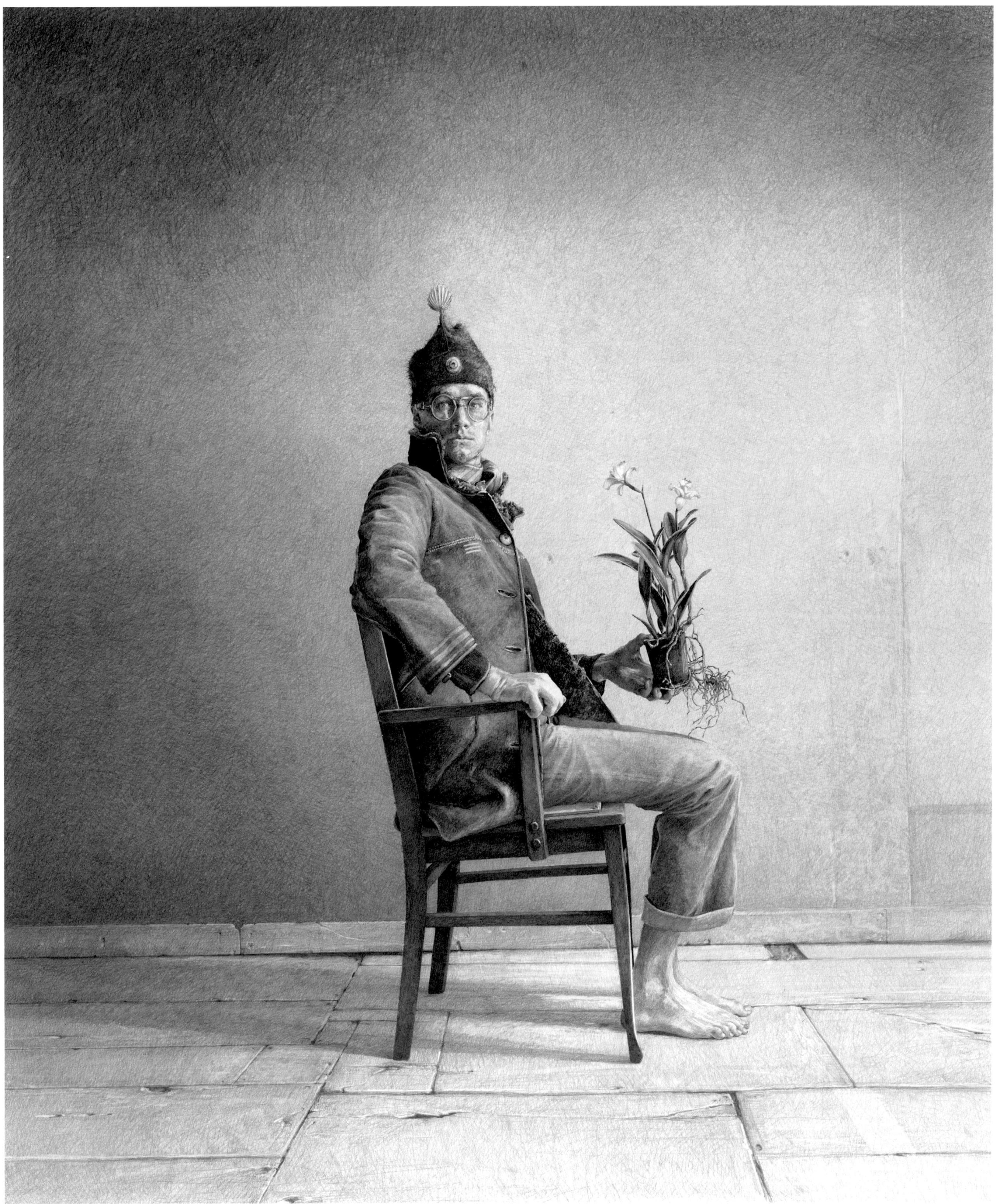

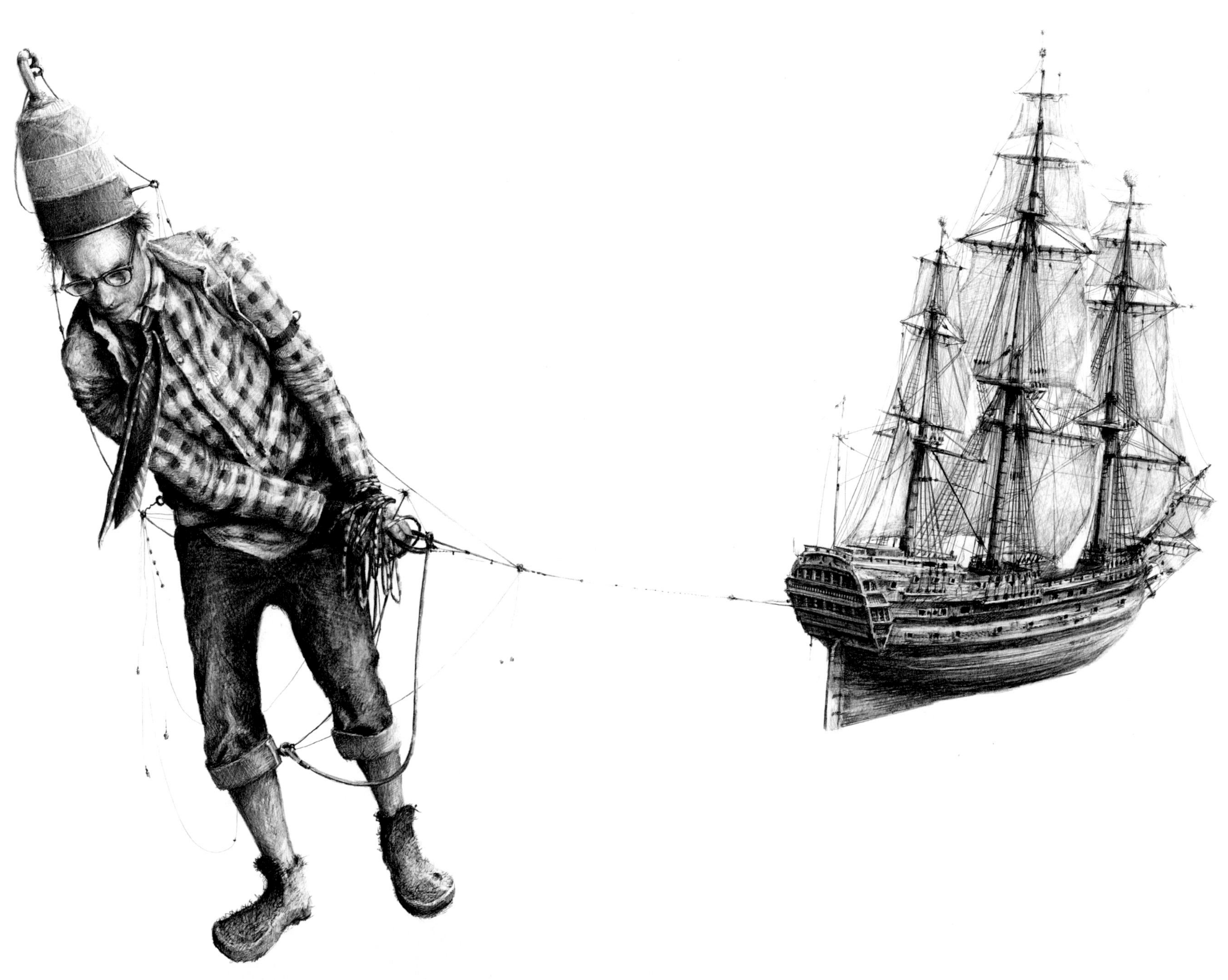

Ethan Murrow was born in Greenfield, Massachusetts in 1975.

He received his B.A. from Carleton College and his M.F.A from The University of North Carolina, Chapel Hill. He shows with Slete Gallery in Los Angeles, Winston Wächter in New York and Seattle, and La Galerie Particulière in Paris and Brussels. He lives in Boston, Massachusetts and serves on the Graduate and Painting Faculty at the School of the Museum of Fine Arts.

*Same Echo*, detail

## Introduction

p. 7: *Pluto* Installation view, permanent piece. Sharpie on wall. Facebook Boston offices.

## The One and the Many

p. 8: *Washington D.C.* Installation view. Ballpoint pen on wall, Winston Wächter Fine Art, New York City, NY, spring 2014.

p. 11: *Doodlebugging* Installation view, permanent piece. Sharpie on wood set in concrete under glass. Winston Wächter Fine Art, Seattle, WA, spring 2015.

pp. 13, 15: *Flotilla* Installation view. Three-story wall drawing in ballpoint pen at the deCordova Museum Biennial, Lincoln, MA, fall 2013.

p. 16: *Seastead* Installation view. Sharpie on wall. Institute of Contemporary Art Boston, Feinberg Art Wall, summer 2015–fall 2016.

## Omniscient Landscapes

p. 19: *Sled Is Responsive, Soft Landing in Doubt* (2009) graphite on paper 70 × 70 in. (178 × 178 cm)

pp. 20–21: *Northwest Passage* (2015) graphite on paper 36 × 60 in. (91 × 152 cm)

p. 23: *Foot Is Still Cramping Up, Results Otherwise Positive* (2009) graphite on paper 36 × 36 in. (91 × 91 cm)

pp. 24–25: *Exit* (2015) graphite on paper 20 × 90 in. (51 × 229 cm)

p. 27: *Appleseed* (2014) graphite on paper 68 × 68 in. (173 × 173 cm)

p. 29: *Early Warning System* (2013) graphite on paper 36 × 36 in. (91 × 91 cm)

p. 31: *Rebellion* (2014) graphite on paper 48 × 48 in. (122 × 122 cm)

p. 32: *The Old Aristocratic Colors Breaking Through* (2013) graphite on paper 48 × 48 in. (121 × 121 cm)

p. 33: *Influx* (2015) graphite on paper 36 × 36 in. (91 × 91 cm)

p. 35: *State of Alaska* (2014) graphite on paper 36 × 36 in. (91 × 91 cm)

p. 37: *Moby Dick* (2013) graphite on paper 48 × 48 in. (122 × 122 cm)

pp. 38–39: *Albert Bierstadt* (2013) graphite on paper 48 × 66 in. (122 × 168 cm)

p. 41: *Fiefdom* (2015) graphite on paper 52 × 42 in. (132 × 107 cm)

pp. 42–43: *Napoleon Custer Mithradetes of Whitehall* (2011) graphite on paper 30 × 120 in. (76 × 305 cm)

p. 45: *Nueva Iguarán* (2014) graphite on paper 36 × 36 in. (91 × 91 cm)

p. 47: *Water Guard* (2014) graphite on paper 68 × 68 in. (173 × 173 cm)

p. 49: *Expansion* (2014) graphite on paper 36 × 36 in. (91 × 91 cm)

p. 51: *Ellesmere Island Tar Pit* (2014) graphite on paper 48 × 48 in. (121 × 121 cm)

p. 53: *State of Massachusetts* (2014) graphite on paper 48 × 48 in. (122 × 122 cm)

p. 55: *Decide Nothing* (2011) graphite on paper 36 × 36 in. (91 × 91 cm)

## Prosceniums

p. 57: *Captains of Revision* (2013) graphite on paper
42 × 42 in. (107 × 107 cm)

p. 59: *State of Nevada* (2014) graphite on paper 48 × 48 in. (122 × 122 cm)

pp. 60–61: *Alibi* (2011) graphite on paper 36 × 48 in. (91 × 122 cm)

p. 63: *State of Texas* (2014) graphite on paper 48 × 48 in. (122 × 122 cm)

pp. 64–65: *Agitprop* (2014) graphite on paper 36 × 48 in. (91 × 122 cm)

p. 67: *Jenga Housing Scheme* (2011) graphite on paper
48 × 48 in. (122 × 122 cm)

pp. 68–69: *Make No Parley* (2012) graphite on paper 30 × 60 in. (76 × 152 cm)

pp. 70–71: *State of California* (2014) graphite on paper
30 × 105 in. (76 × 267 cm)

pp. 72–73: *Polyphonic* (2011) graphite on paper 54 × 72 in. (137 × 183 cm)

p. 75: *It Moved Again* (2010) graphite on paper 36 × 36 in. (91 × 91 cm)

pp. 76–77: *General Curtis Méliès* (2015) graphite on paper
48 × 60 in. (122 × 152 cm)

p. 79: *Columbia River Beehive* (2015) graphite on paper
52 × 42 in. (132 × 107 cm)

p. 81: *And They Stirred* (2010) graphite on paper
48 × 48 in. (122 × 122 cm)

## Interior Monologue

p. 83: *Speed Reading Quota Enlarged during Inclement Weather* (2009)
graphite on paper 48 × 48 in. (122 × 122 cm)

pp. 84–85: *The Prisoners* (2010) graphite on paper 20 × 72 in. (51 × 183 cm)

p. 87: *Raw Diet Increasing Audacity and Night Vision* (2009)
graphite on paper 36 × 36 in. (91 × 91 cm)

p. 89: *Obelix* (2012) graphite on paper 28 × 28 in. (71 × 71 cm)

pp. 90–91: *Negligible Frostnip during Baffin Bay Freefall* (2008)
graphite on paper 38 × 78 in. (97 × 198 cm)

p. 93: *An Iron Roller Coaster Rose Out of the Tundra and Quite a Few Wondered Why but No One Said a Word* (2010) graphite on paper
48 × 48 in. (122 × 122 cm)

pp. 94–95: *Error* (2011) graphite on paper 20 × 36 in. (51 × 91 cm)

p. 97: *Crimean War* (2012) graphite on paper 36 × 36 in. (91 × 91 cm)

p. 99: *Will Be Snaring Meteorites – And See Infinite Possibility Controlled* (2010) graphite on paper 48 × 48 in. (122 × 122 cm)

p. 100: *Will Be Snaring Meteorites – And Win the War Game of the Sky* (2010)
graphite on paper 48 × 48 in. (122 × 122 cm)

p. 101: *Will Be Snaring Meteorites – And Build a Library of Success* (2010)
graphite on paper 48 × 48 in. (122 × 122 cm)

p. 103: *Paranoia* (2012) graphite on paper 36 × 36 in. (91 × 91 cm)

p. 105: *Fresh and Strong the World We Seize* (2011) graphite on paper
96 × 52 in. (244 × 132 cm)

p. 107: *Narcissus* (2012) graphite on paper 36 x 41 in. (91 × 104 cm)

p. 109: *Himself Mourning Himself Made for an Awkward Wake* (2010)
graphite on paper 36 × 36 in. (91 × 91 cm)

pp. 110–111: *The Furnace* (2011) graphite on paper 20 × 36 in. (51 × 91 cm)

p. 113: *To Atlantis* (2015) graphite on paper 36 × 36 in. (91 × 91 cm)

p. 115: *He Chose to Raise Orchids, and Spurned Catherine the Great's Advances* (2010) graphite on paper 68 × 58 in. (173 × 147 cm)

p. 116: *Same Echo* (2011) graphite on paper 48 × 48 in. (122 × 122 cm)

# Ethan Murrow

Copyediting: Aaron Bogart
Graphic design: Hannes Aechter
Typeface: Graphik
Project management: Cassandra Edlefsen Lasch, Hatje Cantz
Production: Heidrun Zimmermann, Hatje Cantz
Reproductions: Jan Scheffler, prints professional
Printing: Offsetdruckerei Karl Grammlich GmbH, Pliezhausen
Paper: LuxoArt Samt, 150 g/m²
Binding: Lachenmaier GmbH, Reutlingen

Thanks to Ray Azoulay, Stacey Winston Levitan, Christine Wächter Campbell, Frédéric Biousse, Guillame Foucher, Clements Photo, and Vita Murrow

With the generous support of Slete Gallery, Los Angeles; Winston Wächter Fine Art, New York and Seattle; La Galerie Particulière, Paris and Brussels



Published by
Hatje Cantz Verlag
Zeppelinstrasse 32
73760 Ostfildern
Germany
Tel. +49 711 4405-200
Fax +49 711 4405-220
www.hatjecantz.com

A Ganske Publishing Group company
Hatje Cantz books are available internationally at selected bookstores.
For more information about our distribution partners, please visit our website at www.hatjecantz.com.

ISBN 978-3-7757-4050-0

Printed in Germany

Cover illustration: *Negligible Frostnip during Baffin Bay Freefall*